CLAIT PLUS

OCR LEVEL 2 CERTIFICATE FOR IT USERS

VERONICA WHITE

PENNY HILL

Heinemann

OCR
RECOGNISING ACHIEV

Heinemann Educational Publishers
Halley Court, Jordan Hill, Oxford, OX2 8EJ
Part of Harcourt Education

Heinemann is the registered trademark of Harcourt Education Ltd

First published in 2002
2005 2004 2003
10 9 8 7 6 5 4 3

A catalogue record for this book is available from the British Library on request.

IBSN 0 435 45082 4

Designed and typeset by Artistix
Printed and bound in Spain by Edelvives

Tel: 01865 888058 www.heinemann.co.uk

Acknowledgements

Veronica White would like to thank Norman Dyer for his assistance at the start of this project, and Melanie and Angelo (Millas Magical Circus) who inspired the theme for the assignments.

As this is the end of an era, I would also like to thank those with whom I have had the pleasure of working on the "old" schemes over the years. The guiding light for all the years was Sara Coldicott. There have been many scheme officers but Peter West and Clem Burke were outstanding colleagues. On the IT Schemes Committee, John Bayliss chaired many challenging hours of debate.

My thanks for the help and support of Pat Lusty, Amanda Howell, Cath Smith and Ros Howarth.

On the IBTII scheme, my thanks go to all the Marking Co-ordinators, but especially the regionals – Linda Clark, Jenny Collyer and George Macdonald.

AND FINALLY . . .

Pen Gresford who has supported and encouraged me through so many testing times and Alex Gray for his calm, soothing style (and great editing).

The publishers wish to acknowledge that the screenshots in this book have been reprinted with kind permission from Microsoft Corporation.

Contents

UNIT 1 Create, Manage and Integrate Files   10

UNIT 2 Spreadsheets   34

UNIT 3 Databases   46

UNIT 4 Desktop Publishing   64

UNIT 5 Presentation Graphics   84

Introduction
The CLAIT PLUS Applications

The scheme

The OCR Level 2 Certificate for IT Users (CLAIT PLUS) is designed to develop the skills, knowledge and understanding that an IT user might need in employment, education or training.

CLAIT PLUS has been developed from, and replaces, IBT II, Databases II, Spreadsheets II, Desktop Publishing II, Desktop Publishing III and Cambridge Information Technology. It follows on from New CLAIT.

To achieve a full certificate qualification, candidates are required to achieve four units: the mandatory core unit plus three additional optional units.

Certification is also available at unit level. Each unit is regarded as a worthwhile achievement in its own right. Candidates have the option of achieving as many, or as few, units as are appropriate for their own learning needs or employment situation.

The mandatory core unit has been designed to encompass the essential core knowledge and competencies that are needed in the workplace to complete both routine and non-routine tasks. The optional units allow candidates to develop skills in a range of different IT applications.

The scheme aims to develop:

- knowledge of IT hardware and software and their correct and safe operation
- knowledge and use of a range of software applications to complete complex tasks
- ability to manage and manipulate complex documents and data in a variety of applications
- ability to manipulate and integrate data across different applications
- ability to enter data accurately
- skills and knowledge in contexts that are directly relevant to employment situations.

The units in OCR's Level 2 Certificate for IT Users (CLAIT PLUS) are:

Unit 1   Create, Manage and Integrate Files

Unit 2   Spreadsheets

Unit 3   Databases

Unit 4   Desktop Publishing

Unit 5   Presentation Graphics

Unit 6   Computer Art

Unit 7   Web Page Creation

Unit 8   Electronic Communication

Unit 9   Graphs and Charts

Unit 10   Spreadsheet Solutions

Unit 11   Database Solutions

Unit 12   Desktop Publishing Solutions

Unit 13   Presentation Graphics Solutions

Unit 14   Digital Imaging Solutions

Unit 15   Web Animation Solutions

Unit 16   Weg Page Solutions

Unit 17   Word Processing
          (Microsoft Office Specialist Word Core)

Unit 18   Spreadsheets
          (Microsoft Office Specialist Excel Core)

Unit 19   Databases
          (Microsoft Office Specialist Access Core)

Unit 20   Presentation Graphics
          (Microsoft Office Specialist PowerPoint Core/Comprehensive)

Unit 21   Electronic Communication
          (Microsoft Office Specialist Outlook Core)

Unit content

Full details of the OCR syllabus can be found on the CD that accompanies this book. Each unit is structured as follows:

Description
The skills the unit is designed to cover.

Learning outcomes
What you can expect to know having followed a course to prepare you for this unit.

Recommended prior learning
What you need to know before you begin. It is advisable to cover the equivalent Level 1 unit. It is also helpful to cover the core unit first as some of the skills for the other units are included in the core.

Entry restrictions
Units that cannot be submitted for the full certificate – eg, Unit 2 Spreadsheets, Unit 10 Spreadsheet Solutions, or Unit 18 Spreadsheets (Microsoft Specialist Excel Core).

Assessment
How assessment is carried out, the length of the test, and who marks your work (ie OCR or your tutor).

Unit content
What you need to know before you start the test (knowledge and understanding) and what will be tested (assessment objectives).

Marking criteria
How your work will be marked.

The book

The book is designed to guide you through Units 1 to 9 of the scheme. Neither the solutions units nor the Microsoft Office Specialist units are covered. It will introduce you to the skills required to undertake assessment at Level 2. It assumes that you will have undertaken the Level I unit in the same application.

The guidance given is *one way only* of carrying out the requirements of the assessment objectives. There will be other ways. For the purposes of this book, the instructions given are using Microsoft Windows 98 and Office 2000. If you are not using this software combination, you will need to refer to your computer manual to find out the exact instructions for your machine.

How To Use This Book

This book is set out in units. Each unit can be used independently of the others and you can use them in any order. In each unit you will find:

An introduction
This includes a guide to what you will cover in the unit, and how your work will be marked. There is also a guide on how to meet the assessment objectives.

Build up exercises
These introduce you to the requirements of the scheme within the unit, and together provide a practice assignment. In this File they are all based on one theme – a children's entertainment company, Creativity.

On the CD that comes with this book you will find:
The unit content (or syllabus)

A checklist
This is for you to complete to form a reference sheet.

Specimen assignments
These will provide assessment practice. All the units are based on one theme – a delivery service, Del's Doorstep Deli.

All the tasks have numbers printed down the left-hand side. They relate to the assessment objectives in the CLAIT PLUS scheme for which this book is written.

Note: The assignments in this book and on the CD are not to be used as the final assessment. They are intended as practice assignments only.

Tutor's Resource File

There is a Tutor's Resource File (also published by Heinemann Educational) that accompanies this student book. Your tutor may have that File and will be able to give you more assignments for any of the applications you may wish to gain.

How will you be assessed?

You will be assessed in the practical use of software applications by completing practical assignments. All units are equally weighted. Neither the full certificate nor the individual units are graded. You are permitted one attempt only at each assignment. If you are not successful, you may attempt a **different** assignment.

The core unit is marked by an OCR examiner-moderator. All optional units are marked by your tutor and then checked by an OCR examiner-moderator. Computer-based assessment is to be made available to all centres for the most popular units of the scheme.

How many applications are you required to do?

The scheme is designed to be flexible. There is no requirement to work towards the units in any particular order. You can attempt any number of the units from just one to all. You may choose the units that reflect your own needs or interests.

To gain a full certificate you are required to achieve four units, the core (Unit 1) plus three optional units. Units may be achieved and certificated separately.

The core unit, Unit 1 Create, Manage and Integrate Files, is tested by a three-hour OCR-set assignment and is marked by OCR. Units 2–9 are all tested by a three-hour OCR-set assignment, and marked by your tutor and then moderated by OCR. Units 10–16 (the Solutions units) are tested by locally devised tasks, which are marked by your tutor, and then moderated by OCR. The Microsoft Office Specialists units are also self-contained modules subject to computer-based assessment only.

Restrictions

There are restrictions within the scheme. The main restriction is that you cannot submit both a unit and its **Solutions** or **Microsoft Office Specialist** equivalent (eg Spreadsheets, Spreadsheet Solutions and Spreadsheets Microsoft Office Specialist Excel Core) as separate units for the full certificate.

How can you be successful?

The syllabus clearly identifies the work you will have to do. You should complete the assignments with no **critical** errors, and not more than three **accuracy** errors. The critical errors, which are different for each unit, are identified at the beginning of the respective units.

You may use English and mother-tongue dictionaries, spellcheckers (UK English), centre-prepared manuals or manufacturers' manuals during the assessment.

As the award of a CLAIT PLUS Certificate makes a direct claim about a candidate's readiness for employment, the assessment objectives must be met each time they are specified. Unlike New CLAIT, errors cannot be 'corrected later'.

Accuracy errors

An accuracy error is one that does not prevent the document from being used, and may occur in two different ways:

- an error in completing an assessment objective
- an error in keying data (a data entry error).

In CLAIT PLUS, no distinction is made between these two types of error, and both types count equally towards the overall total of **three** permitted accuracy errors per assignment.

Data entry errors

A data entry error is an incorrect, omitted, or superfluous character in a data item or an omitted or superfluous space. Only one data entry error should be counted for a data item, regardless of the number of errors in the data item. Details of data items are shown at the beginning of each unit.

What certificate will you get?

If you achieve the core unit (Unit 1) plus three optional units you will be awarded an OCR Level 2 Certificate for IT Users (CLAIT PLUS), listing the units achieved. Candidates who achieve fewer than the number of units required for a full qualification will be awarded a unit certificate for each unit achieved.

The CD

The accompanying CD contains all the files that you will need to complete the units in this book.

It also contains the content (syllabus), a checklist and a further practice assignment for each unit.

Accessing the CD

1. Insert the CD into your CD drive.
2. From the Windows desktop **Start** menu, select **Run**.
3. The **Run** dialogue box is displayed.
4. In the Open box, key in the name of your CD drive – eg D:
5. Click on **OK**.
6. The CD contents will be displayed.
7. Double click on the folder or file that you want to access. If the file is contained in a folder you will need to open the folder (by double-clicking on it to display the file name).
8. Right-click on the file.
9. Select **Copy** from the menu.
10. Click on the down arrow of the **Address** box and click on the destination location.
11. Right-click in a white space in the destination location window.
12. Select **Paste** from the menu.

Files on the CD

The files for each unit are stored in a folder indicating that unit – eg the files for Unit 1 Create, Manage and Integrate Files are in the folder Unit 1.

You will be told within each task the name of the file (or files) that you must use.

CD Files

Unit	Task	Folder	Folder	Files		
Unit 1	Overview	Unit 1		INFORM.TXT DOG.JPG	FILEDATA.MBD	SSGRAPH.XLS
	Task 1	Unit 1 Unit 1 Unit 1	creclow clowoth clowoth	clowns.txt partypie.xls creative.jpg	fancy.csv	
	Practice assignment 1	Unit 1		LETTER.TXT WINNER.JPG	SALES.XLS	NEWTEL.CSV
Unit 2	Task 1	Unit 2		runcost.csv		
	Task 3	Unit 2		costings.csv		
	Practice assignment 1	Unit 2		VEHICLE.CSV	PERCENT.CSV	
Unit 3	Overview	Unit 3		sample.mbd	sample examples.mbd	
	Task 3	Unit 3		cusfile.csv		
	Practice assignment 1	Unit 3		DELIVER.CSV		
Unit 4	Task 1	Unit 4		birth.txt	bigfoot.gif	strip.gif
	Practice assignment 1	Unit 4		MARCH.TXT BASKET.JPG	VOUCHER.TXT VAN.JPG	NOTE.BMP CALZONE.JPG
Unit 5	Task 1	Unit 5		clopres.txt	cloim.gif	
	Task 3			clospeak.txt		
	Practice assignment 1	Unit 5		COOK.GIF HYGIENE.TXT	SAFETY NOTES.TXT	
Unit 6	Task 1	Unit 6		clouds.gif maestro3.gif	maestro2.gif logo.gif	dmaestro.gif
	Task 2	Unit 6		flower.gif	sax.gif	finger.gif
	Practice assignment 1	Unit 6		SHOP.JPG	DELIVAN.JPG	COOK.JPG
Unit 7	Overview	Unit 7 Unit 7 Unit 7	sampleweb images _vti_cnf	first page.htm frog.gif frog.gif		
	Task 1	Unit 7		bookword.txt homepage.txt emailus.gif booking.gif rocky.gif	feedback.txt home.gif clowns.gif saxman.jpg balls.gif	feedback.gif package.txt balloons.gif maestro.gif clownkid.gif
	Practice assignment 1	Unit 7		index.txt abt.gif list.txt dels.gif salads.gif flan.gif	BGRDY.GIF events.txt event.gif newprem.gif kebab.gif	company.txt prod.gif meal.gif mail.gif fruits.gif
Unit 8	Task 1	Unit 8		prestext.txt	avail.csv	clownad.gif
	Practice assignment 1	Unit 8		DETAILS.CSV	DANGER.JPG	TEMPER.TXT
Unit 9	Task 1	Unit 9		split.csv		
	Task 2	Unit 9		split.csv		
	Task 3	Unit 9		ttlbooks.csv		
	Task 4	Unit 9		ttlbooks.csv		
	Practice assignment 1	Unit 9		WRAPDATA.CSV SPEVDATA.CSV	SALEDATA.CSV VANDATA.CSV	NONSDATA.CSV

UNIT 1 Create, Manage and Integrate Files

This unit is designed to test your ability to use a computer to create and manage different file types from a variety of sources (eg, database, spreadsheet) to produce a business document. You will create folders and files and enter data from source documents.

You may find it easier to undertake this unit if you have completed the following units at Level 1 – Using a Computer, Databases, Spreadsheets, Word Processing and Graphs and Charts. If you have done so, you will already know how to:

- identify and use a computer system and application software correctly
- locate and access data on a computer
- format, search for, and sort data
- manage documents and data
- print graphs, database and spreadsheet files and word processing documents.

To pass this unit

You must complete the three-hour OCR-set assignment without making any critical errors, and with no more than three accuracy errors. Your work for this unit will be marked by OCR.

If you do not achieve a Pass you may re-take the assessment using a **different** assignment.

Critical errors

- The data file is missing or incomplete.
- The spreadsheet chart is missing or incomplete.
- The image is missing or incomplete.
- The document printout is incomplete.

Accuracy errors

- Each instance of an error in entering data. In this unit apply one data entry error for any error(s) in any word.
- Each instance of an error in completing an assessment objective.

What will you learn?

When you have completed this unit you should be able to:

- use a computer's system software safely and securely
- create and manage files and folders
- use an input device to enter data accurately from a variety of sources
- work with data files using database and/or spreadsheet software to select and import data
- create and print an integrated document, combining text, numeric and tabular data, an image and a chart
- format a document using a house style.

How to meet the assessment objectives

You will be introduced to **one** method of achieving the assessment objectives. There will be other methods of carrying out these tasks. Only objectives that were not covered in Level 1 are included.

You will already know how to use a computer system and application software correctly (ie word processing, database and spreadsheet), locate and access data on a computer, search for and sort data. You will also be familiar with formatting data, managing documents and data, and printing graphs, database and spreadsheet files and word processed documents.

You will now cover the new skills in this unit. Many of these will also be needed for the other units, such as copying files into folders.

For this series of tasks you will be working with folders and files. You can find them on the CD supplied with this book.

Now we will deal with the new areas.

Managing files and folders

Opening your working area

Load your system. Locate the **My Computer** icon.

Click on the right mouse button.

A drop down menu will appear. Click **Open**.

Preparing your work area

You have to locate *your* working area. The working area that will be used in these tasks will be **C:**. Ask your tutor which area you should use.

Place your mouse over the **(C:)** icon.

Click on the right mouse button.

Click **Open**.

Creating a new folder

In your working area, click **File, New, Folder**.

Naming a folder

New Folder is highlighted, with the cursor at the end of the name.

Name your folder **claplus** and press Enter.

Renaming a folder

Locate the folder you want to rename – **claplus**.

Right click on the folder. Click **Rename**.

Enter the new name for the folder – **Practice**.

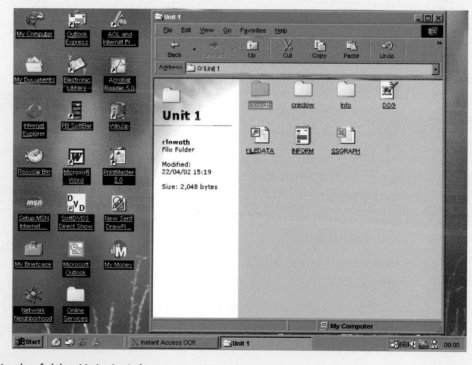

Opening folders and copying files

Now you are going to copy files.

Click on **My Computer** icon.

Position your mouse on the blue bar at the top of the open window and hold down the left mouse button. Move the window to the right of the screen.

Locate the area in which your working files have been stored (your CD-ROM drive). In this exercise it is Q – the files are stored on **Q:** in the folder **Unit 1**. Ask your tutor which drive you should use.

Click on the icon for **your CD-ROM** drive, then **Unit 1**.

Click on the **My Computer** icon again.

To go to your working area, click the **(C:)** icon.

Locate your **Practice** folder and click on the icon.

Move this window to the left of the screen. Reduce the width of the windows so that both are clearly visible.

The files you are going to copy are shown in the **Unit 1** window. They are **INFORM**, **SSGRAPH**, **FILEDATA** and **DOG**.

You will copy them into the **Practice** folder.

To do this you need to select the files.

Move to the first file – DOG – and click on the left mouse button.

The file will now have a blue background.

Holding down the **Ctrl** key, move to the next file **SSGRAPH** and click.

The background for this file will now also be blue.

With the **Ctrl** key still held down, repeat this action until the four files have a blue background.

Place your mouse over any of the files with the blue background.

In the exercise the mouse has been placed over the file DOG.

Click on the right mouse button. Click on **Copy**.

Move to the open **Practice** window on the left of the screen.

Click on the right mouse button, then **Paste**.

The files have now been copied and you can close the windows.

Move to the **X** button located on the blue bar in the top right of the window.

Click on the left mouse button and the window will close.

Repeat this action to close the second window.

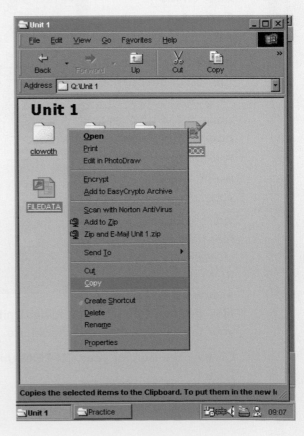

Copying a folder

It is important to have backup copies of your files. You are going to make a copy of your **Practice** folder.

In **C:** Click on your **Practice** folder.

Right click on your mouse.

Click **Copy**.

Click **Paste**.

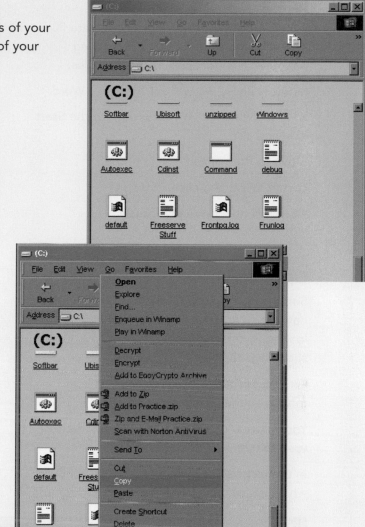

A new folder will be created for you called **Copy of Practice**.
It contains a copy of all the files in **Practice**.

Close **C:**.

Loading a program

In Unit 1 Create, Manage and Integrate Files you will need to use a word processing package to import and manipulate files.

In this exercise we will use Microsoft Word.

To load **Word**, move your mouse to the **Start** icon and click.

Move to **Programs**.

Locate **Word** and click.

Word will now be ready for use.

Opening an existing file

Some of the files with which you will work have been saved in a format that can be loaded in different operating systems. One such file is the text file **INFORM**.

To load this file into Word, position your mouse on the **Open** icon and click.

You will now need to locate the file that you wish to open.

In this exercise you will open the file **INFORM**, which is saved in your **Practice** folder.

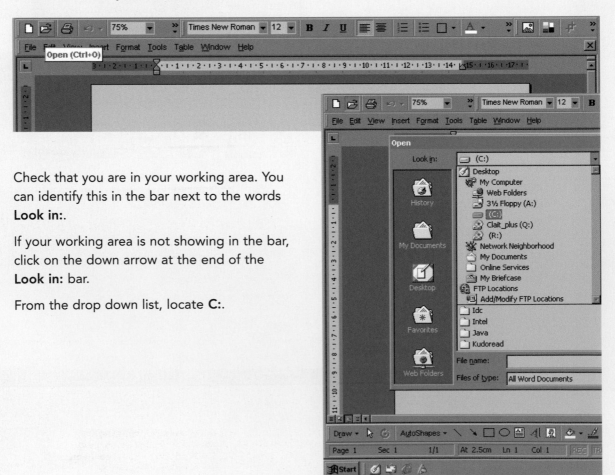

Check that you are in your working area. You can identify this in the bar next to the words **Look in:**.

If your working area is not showing in the bar, click on the down arrow at the end of the **Look in:** bar.

From the drop down list, locate **C:**.

From C: open the **Practice** folder, containing the **INFORM** file.

The file you want to open Is not a Word file, and it may not be shown in the window.

At the bottom of the window you will see a bar **Files of type**:.

To show all your files, go to the down arrow at the end of the bar and click **All files**.

The filename **INFORM** will now be displayed.

Go to the file icon and click to select the file.

Press **Enter**.

Your file will now be open and ready for use.

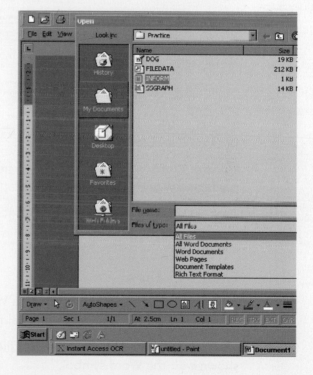

Saving a file as a Word document

Go to **File** on the menu bar and click. A drop down menu will appear.

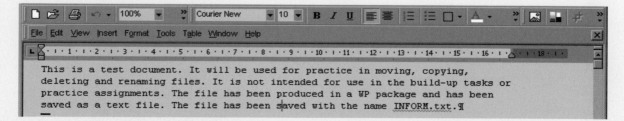

Go to **Save As:** and click.

The **Save As** menu will appear.

At the bottom of the window you will see the **Save as type:** bar.

Click on the down arrow at the end of this bar.

Find **Word Document** and click.

Click on the **Save** button.

Your document will now be saved as a Word document.

Closing files and programs

To close the file **INFORM** –

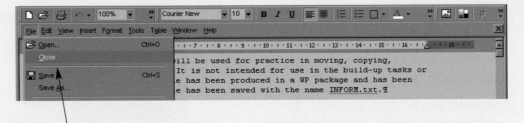

Click on **File, Close**.

To close Word, go to the **X** at the far right of the blue bar at the top of the screen.

Click on the **X**.

Deleting files

Now that you have saved the file as a Word document, you can delete the original file.

Open your **Practice** folder. Your new file is shown with the Word symbol.

To select your file, go to the **text** file **INFORM**.

Click on the right mouse button.

Click on **Delete**.

You will be asked to confirm removal of the file.

The text file will now be deleted.

Moving files and folders

As you have finished working in the **Practice** folder, you can move the new Word document into the folder containing your backup files – **Copy of Practice**.

Open both folders.

Go to the Word file **INFORM**. Click on the right mouse button, click on **Cut**.

Go to the **Copy of Practice** folder. Click on the right mouse button, click on **Paste**.

The document will have been moved from the **Practice** to the **Copy of Practice** folder.

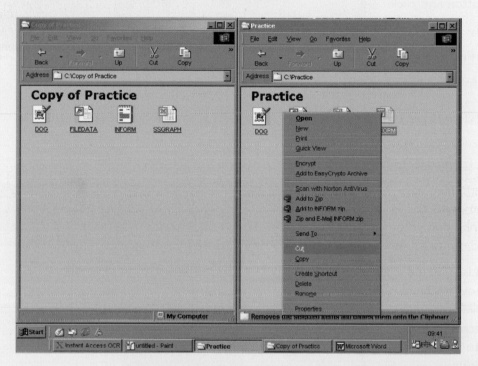

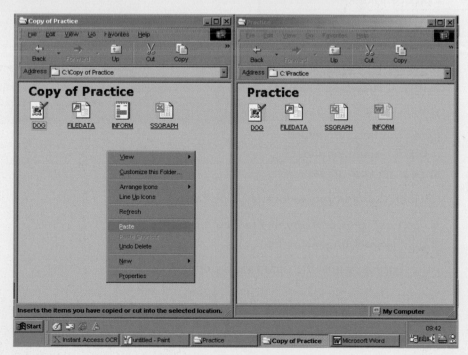

Deleting folders

A folder can be deleted in the same way as a file.

Note: If you delete a **folder** you will also delete all the **files** in that folder.

You no longer need the **Practice** folder. To delete it you must close it so that you can see the **Practice** folder in the window.

In the **Practice** folder go to the **Back** button and click.

This will take you to **C:**.

Go to your **Practice** folder.

Delete the folder in the same way that you deleted a file.

Making screen prints

You will often need to make screen prints to show evidence that you have carried out tasks.

In this exercise you are going to show evidence that you have copied the files, and moved the Word document to the **Copy of Practice** folder.

Open the **Copy of Practice** folder.

Press the key marked **PrtScr** or **PrintScrn** on your keyboard.

Open the Program **Word**. A blank document should appear on your screen.

Click on the right mouse button, click **Paste**.

A "picture" of your **Copy of Practice** folder should appear on your screen.

Add your name and the date to this printout.

You can do this by keying it in directly onto the page or adding it as a header or a footer.

Save and close your file and Word.

House style

Format page layout

To change the **Orientation**, click **File**, **Page Setup** and **Paper Size**. Select Portrait or Landscape.

To change the **Margins**, click **File**, **Page Setup** and **Margins**. Make any changes you require.

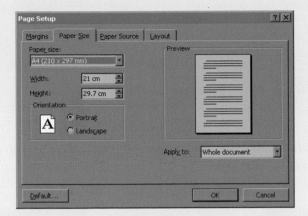

To insert a Header or Footer, including the use of automatic fields (filename, page no, date), click **View**.

Select **Header and Footer**. You can then enter the data.

To enter automatic fields, go to the position where you want the data to appear and click on the relevant icon. If you cannot see the automatic field you want, click **Insert AutoText**.

Click on the **Close** button to exit.

Numbering text or items

To apply numbering select the data to which the feature is to be applied. Click on the Numbering icon. Numbers will be applied to the highlighted text.

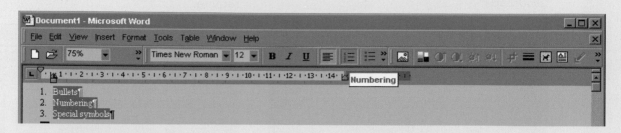

To change the Numbering style, click **Format**, **Bullets and Numbering**, **Numbered**. Select a style or **Customise**.

You can create your own style using this screen.

Applying bullets to text or items

To apply bullets, select the data to which the feature is to be applied. Click on the Bullets icon. The feature will be applied to the highlighted text.

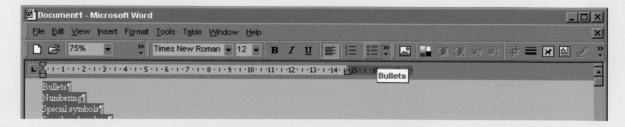

To change the Bullets style click **Format**, **Bullets and Numbering, Bulleted**. Select a style or **Customise**.

You can create your own style using this screen.

Inserting a table

To insert a table: on the Toolbar click **Table**, **Insert, Table**. You can now specify the number of columns and rows that you require, as well as selecting the column width or autofit.

To close, and enter data, click **OK**.

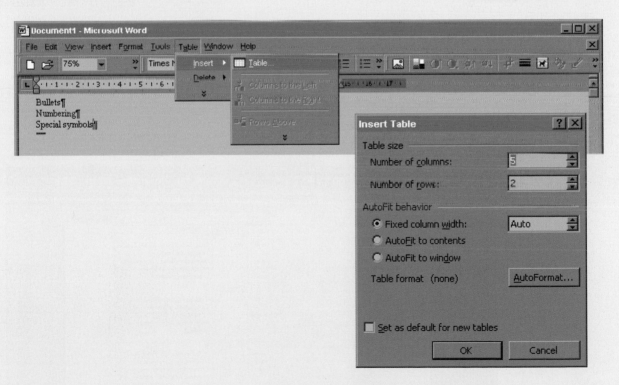

Applying gridlines, borders or shading to a table

Gridlines are inserted as the default in Tables. To change the style, highlight the table.

Staff No	Name	Department
32	Dyer	Purchasing
35	White	Accounts

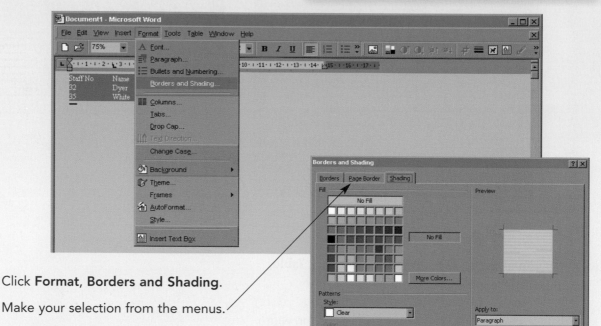

Click **Format, Borders and Shading**.

Make your selection from the menus.

- **Borders**
- **Page Border**
- **Shading**

Use spellcheck facilities

Click **Tools, Spelling and Grammar**.

Read the information on the screen regarding each word being checked, eg the suggested options or choices of words, or perhaps the word is a 'repeated' word.

Use special symbols

To select symbols or special characters.

Click **Insert**, **Symbol**.

You can then select the required symbol or character.

Click **Insert**, **Close**.

Importing files

To bring a file or image into your document click **Insert**.

You will then have the options of

Picture

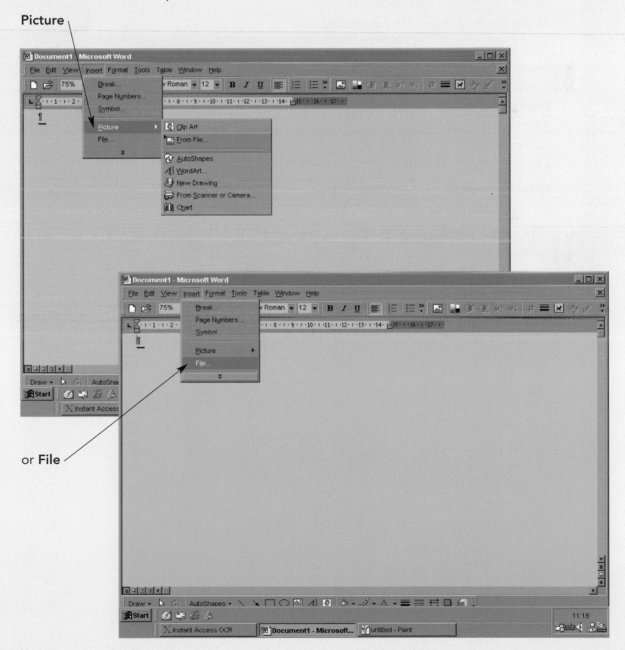

or **File**

Specify the source of the file.

Select the file from the list.

Click **Insert**.

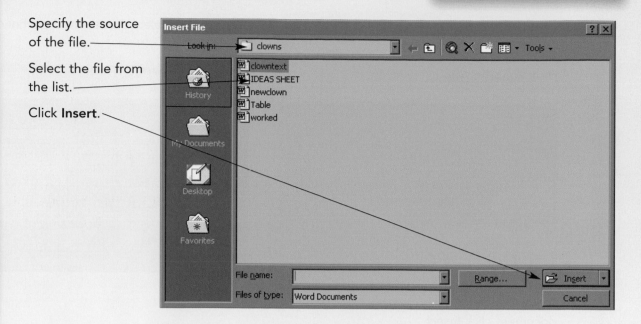

Search and replace

To use the Search and Replace facility.

Click **Edit**, **Replace**. On the Replace tab in the **Find What**: box enter the word(s) to be replaced.

In the **Replace With**: box enter the new word(s).

Click on the **More** button to select further options.

Build Up Exercises

TASK 1

This task is designed to allow you to practise some of the skills required to gain the OCR Level 2 Certificate for IT Users (CLAIT PLUS) assessment objectives for Unit 1 Create, Manage and Integrate Files. To cover all the assessment objectives you will also have to complete Task 2.

Before you begin

You should know how to:

- manage files and folders
- enter data from input sheets into a table
- apply a house style sheet
- print a document.

Scenario

You are working for an entertainment company that organises parties and shows for children. A document has been prepared that can be updated and sent to people who enquire about the services provided. You are required to make the necessary changes to the document to incorporate the latest details.

In this task you will create folders and copy files from the CD accompanying this book into one of them. You will also create a new file and enter a table.

When you undertake the assignment you will have to enter a table into the document you are creating from source documents.

For the purposes of these tasks, you will create and save the table. When you carry out the other practice task you will copy this file into your document. This will not be necessary in the full assignment.

You will need to refer to the:

- Costume Ideas Sheet
- House Style Sheet

What You Have To Do

Assessment Objectives		
1a	1	Create a new folder and call it **finclown**.
1a	2	Within this folder create a new folder and call it **showtime**.
1e	3	Copy the files below from the CD accompanying this book to the folder **showtime**:

Folder:	**creclow**	Filename:	**clowns**
Folder:	**clowoth**	Filename:	**partypie, fancy, creative**

What You Have To Do

Assessment Objectives		
2a, 2c, 5a, 5b, 5c, 5d	4	You are going to create a table. You will need 4 columns. The information is shown on the attached Costume Ideas Sheet. Look at the data before you begin to identify the number of rows that will be required. You must only include the clown characters that are 'cheery'. Use the headings TYPE, MAKEUP, COLOUR and COSTUME. COLOUR should be coded: White – **W**, and Colourful – **C**. Ensure that only the specified data is included and that all the data is visible. You must display gridlines/borders.
4e	5	Apply the relevant section of the house style to the table.
1b	6	Save your file using the name **table**, in the folder **showtime**.
1b, 3e, 3f	7	Print your file and then close it.

TASK 2

Before you begin

You should know how to:

- manage files and folders
- create an integrated document by importing text and graphic files
- amend existing data
- apply a house style sheet.

To produce the document you will need the following files:

A text file with a draft of the document that you will add to, amend, and into which you will import the files.

Folder: **creclow**
Filename: **clowns**

A spreadsheet containing a chart showing the breakdown of the most popular shows last year.

Folder: **clowoth**
Filename: **partypie**

A data file containing details of the fancy dress hire shops in the area.

Folder: **clowoth**
Filename: **fancy**

A graphic of the company logo.

Folder: **clowoth**
Filename: **creative**

TIP You might find it useful to look at these files before you begin the task to familiarise yourself with the text and images to be used.

You will also need to refer to the:

- House Style Sheet
- Draft Document
- Customer Ideas Sheet

What You Have To Do

Assessment Objectives		
Ib, 3a	1	Open the text file named **clowns** and save it in your software's normal file type using the filename **newclown** in the folder **showtime**.
2a, 2b, 2d, 3c, 3d, 3e, 4a, 4b, 4c, 4d, 4f, 5a, 5b, 5c, 5d	2	Using the file **newclown** and referring to the Draft Document on pages 31–32, make the changes shown. Apply the house style to the document as detailed in the House Style Sheet.
2a, 4g	3	You have just received a call from a local agent giving information about a new web site, including details of the artists on his books. Insert the following text at the beginning of the document, as the **second** paragraph. **For full information on all the artists in this area, you should log on to our site www.funnarts.co.uk. To book any of our entertainers call Melanie Thörmon on 644 5601.**
4h	4	Search the document and replace the word **outfit** with the word **costume** wherever it appears.
2e, 4e	5	Spellcheck your document. Make sure that you have applied all the requirements of the house style, and check that all the corrections have been made. The document should now be ready for use without further checking.
Ib, 3f	6	Save your updated document. Print one copy and close the file.
If	7	Rename as **time2** the folder **showtime**.
Ia, Id	8	In your **finclown** folder create a new folder and name it **playtime**. Move the file called **creative** to this folder.
Ic	9	Within the folder **time2**, delete the file **clowns**.
Ig	10	Produce a screen printout of the contents of the folders: **time2** and **playtime**. Add your name and centre no to this printout.

House Style Sheet – Tasks I and 2

Page setup

- Use A4 paper
- Use portrait orientation
- Margins:

top	2.5 cm
bottom	2.5 cm
left	3.5 cm
right	3 cm

- Header: left aligned — candidate name
- Footer: centre — automatic date field (in English format, eg dd-mm-yy)

  right aligned — automatic page no
- Use single line spacing (except where indicated)

Text style

Feature	Font	Point size	Style	Alignment	
Heading	serif	16	bold	centred	
Body	serif	11		justified	
Bullet text	serif	11	italic	left	
Table (with gridlines)	serif	11	bold	column heading	left
			bold	row heading	left (wrapped)
			bold	text	left (wrapped)
Data file imported text (does not apply to graph/chart)	serif	11		text	left
				numeric	left
Graph/chart text	serif	legible			

- Line spacing between headings, subheadings and paragraphs should be applied consistently.
- Widows and orphans must be avoided.
- Text, images, graphs and lines must not be superimposed on each other.
- Imported data must not be split across pages.
- Graphs/charts must be positioned within the margins.
- Spellcheck all documentation. Specialist words have already been checked and no changes should be made to them.

Draft Document

Insert the graphic creative at the t op of each page, applying centre a lignment.

Thank you for your recent enquiry concerning the services we can provide for your forthcoming party.

Run on

We can provide a range of entertainers (magicians, clowns and tumblers) as well as a wide range of events and shows.

Delete

Last year, we found that the most popular party entertainment was our show featuring clowns:

Insert the pie chart here from the sprea dsheet partypie. Ensure that it is within the margins an d legible. Add a border t o frame the chart

We have found in the past that geusts are often keen to dress for events, but are not sure what to wear or where to go to buy or hire a suitable outfit.

I have outlined the diferent types of clown character, and the typical outfit that each type would wear. This will help your invited geusts to select the outfit that they wish to wear for your event. I trust that this guidence will also encourage your geusts to dress in costume for your party. The information also includes the type of makeup suitable for the differing clown types.

We have introduced a new event into our party repertoire, and we include a sheet outlining this exciting adition to our shows – A DAY AT THE CIRCUS.

Insert a page break here

Insert the file table, that you created in Task 1 here.

Fancy dress outlets in your area include:

Insert the fancy database here.

Insert a page break here

All caps an d centre
Apply the Heading style to this te xt only

A Day at the Circus

There is something magical about the circus. Even in this day and age of computer games and satellite television, the smell of sawdust, the roar of the crowd and the jolly tunes still draw us into its cradle of imagination and thrills. It is a place and time for fun with the clowns, friends and the family – simple fun that is rapidly vanishing from our lives.

Move to this position

Start new paragraph here

As soon as they take their seats "butchers" (as they're known in the show) will begin to distribute goodies including peanuts and candyfloss. The performance itself is conducted by a ringmaster, traditionally attired in colourful top hat and tails. He uses a whistle to signal the start of each new act. A live circus band, heavy on the brass, plays lively music.

A typical circus performance will start with an opening grand parade of performers around the hippodrome track, followed by several displays of juglers and acrobats, tumblers and of course, clowns.

Your children and their friends will be encouraged to take part in the acts, and will be introduced to all of the performers. They will be taught, and must observe circus superstitions:

Never look back during a parade
Never sit on the ring curb facing out
Never whistle in the dressing room
Peacock feathers are bad luck
Accidents happen in threes
Elephants must always have their trunks up in pictures
Hair from the tail of an elephant is good luck

Apply bullets and double linespacing to this section only

Move

We can provide the arena and all the entertainers including the musicians. Imagine your children's faces when the doors open and they are ushered into the Big Top. They will see the performance rings in the middle of the tent, surrounded by a hippodrome track.

Costume Ideas Sheet

Type	Character	Makeup	Colour	Costume
Classic European Whiteface	Artistic, colourful, bright and cheery.	Minimal lining colour to outline the eyes, nose, and mouth. Do not wear a comedy nose, false eyelashes, or large ears.	White	Traditional jump suits of white or coloured material. Generally roomy. Buttons or pompoms should be of a contrasting colour.
Straight Whiteface	Elegant, artistic, colourful, bright and cheery.	Minimal lining colour to outline the eyes, nose, and mouth. Any style and colour wig.	White	Satins, sequins, rhinestones and theatrical fabrics (shiny, beaded, etc.). Shoes can be large or small but should be simple.
Comedy Grotesque Whiteface	Remains in charge, throwing rather than taking the pie.	Use large false eyelashes, a larger mouth design and a clown nose. Features may be outlined in black.	White	Traditional jump suit or brightly coloured shirt and pants. Large comedy shoes.
Auguste	The most cheery, impish and gregarious. Thrives on slapstick.	Highly colourful makeup. Eye area is usually white to produce a wide-eyed expression and to accentuate the mouth. Black or red eyes and mouth.	Colourful	A jacket or coat. Pants could be short, long, or oversize. Choose from a wide selection of colourful plaids, stripes, and polka dots, as well as solid colours. Lots of pockets and accessories.
Tramp	Forlorn and downtrodden.	White makeup is used in the eye and mouth areas to exaggerate otherwise 'dirty' complexion.	Muddy	A dark suit or just shirt and pants made to look old and patched with rags or other materials. A dark, battered hat, tattered shoes and socks.

UNIT 2 Spreadsheets

This unit is designed to test your ability to use spreadsheet software to enter and amend data, use functions and formulae, format and print data.

You may find it easier to undertake this unit if you have completed the Spreadsheets unit at Level 1. If you have done so, you will already know how to:

- identify and use spreadsheet software correctly
- use an input device to enter and edit data accurately
- insert, replicate and format arithmetical formulae
- use common numerical formatting and alignment
- manage and print spreadsheet documents.

To pass this unit

You must complete the three-hour OCR-set assignment without making any critical errors, and with no more than three accuracy errors. If you do not achieve a Pass you may re-take the assessment using a different assignment.

You cannot claim more than one unit from the same application area towards the 3 optional units of the Level 2 qualification, due to an overlap in content – ie you may choose one from Unit 2 Spreadsheets, Unit 10 Spreadsheets Solutions or Unit 18 Spreadsheets (Microsoft Office Specialist Excel Core).

Your work will be marked by your tutor, and externally moderated by OCR.

Critical errors

- Any error in entering numeric data that could be used in calculations.
- Failure to link data from one spreadsheet to another.

- Any formula that produces incorrect results.
- Any function that produces incorrect results.
- Failure to display data in full.
- Incorrect projection results.
- Incorrect sort results.

Accuracy errors

- Each instance of an error in entering data. In this unit apply one data entry error for any error(s) in a cell.
- Each instance of an error in completing an assessment objective.

What will you learn?

When you have completed this unit you should be able to:

- enter, edit and manipulate data
- create formulae and use common functions
- format and present data
- link live data from one spreadsheet to another
- use spreadsheets to solve problems and project results.

How to meet the assessment objectives

You will be introduced to **one** method of achieving the assessment objectives. There will be other methods of carrying out these tasks. Only objectives that were not covered in Level 1 are included.

You will already know how to enter, amend and delete data; enter formulae that produce correct results; replicate formulae into appropriate cells; save and name spreadsheets.

Now we will deal with the new areas.

Open a generic file and save it as an Excel Worksheet

A generic file is one that can be opened by more than one operating system. The generic file type used in this unit is a csv (comma separated values) file. To open the file:

Go to the folder where the file is stored. In this case **clowns**. Click on the icon for the file **runcost**. The icon shows in the box to distinguish the **csv** format from a worksheet.

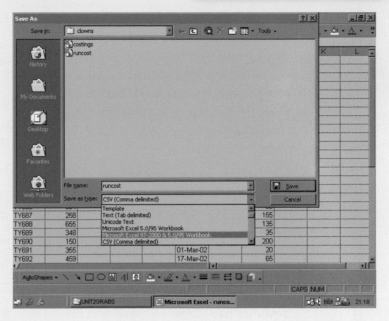

The file will open and you must save it as a Microsoft Excel Workbook.

Enter the name you want to use to save it in the **File name:** box.

Move down to the **Save as type:** box and click the button to view the options.

Highlight Microsoft Excel Workbook.

Click on the Save button.

Your file has now been saved as a Microsoft Excel Workbook with the filename you selected.

Use a range of functions that produce correct results

The functions that may be used in the assignment include SUM, AVERAGE, COUNT, COUNTA or COUNTIF, MIN, MAX, SQRT, IF.

Most of the functions work in the same way:

> Enter the = sign, then the function, then the extent you wish to be included in brackets – eg =SUM(A4:H10) or =AVERAGE(D9:D30) or =MAX(F2:F35).

IF statements are used to test a condition. The condition may be, say, if the value in a cell or range of cells is greater than or less than a specified figure, then a value or remark can be returned in the cell.

Project results

This will normally mean that you will change a value in one cell and note the results of that change on, say, a total in another cell. You will then be required to record that value. You can either enter the figure using the keyboard, or copy the figure (using Paste Special, click **Values** box to ensure that the figure is maintained if the original value is returned).

Use a variety of cell references

You may not have used relative, absolute and mixed cell references. A reference identifies a cell or range of cells. You can use data contained in different cells in one formula or use the value from one cell in several formulas.

- **Relative cell references**
  These are references to cells relative to the position of the formula. They automatically adjust when you copy them. If your formula divides cell B10 with cell B20 (=B10/B20) and you copy the formula to the cell below, both references will be advanced (=B11/B21).

- **Absolute cell references**
  These are references that always refer to cells in a specific location. They do not automatically adjust when you copy them. You can create an absolute reference to a cell by placing a dollar sign ($) before the parts of the reference that you do not wish to change – eg, B3.

You can change relative references to absolute (and vice versa). Select the cell that contains the formula. In the formula bar, select the reference you want to change and then press F4. Each time you press F4, Excel toggles through the combinations:

absolute column and absolute row	(B3)
relative column and absolute row	(B$3)
absolute column and relative row	($B3)
relative column and relative row	(B3)

So, if you select the address B3 in a formula and press F4, the reference becomes B$3. Press F4 again and the reference becomes $B3, and so on.

- **Mixed**

  You may want to advance only part of the reference when you copy a formula. If so, you must use a mixed reference. You can create a mixed reference by placing a dollar sign ($) before the part of the reference that you do not wish to change – eg, $B10.

Naming cells

You will have to know how to name a cell, and how to use that named cell. To name a cell:

With your spreadsheet open, go to the cell you want to name. Click **Insert**, **Name**, **Define**.

You can now enter the name for the cell.

To use a named cell simply enter the name you defined rather than a cell reference.

Linking cells

You will have to use a reference to a cell in another spreadsheet, or 'link'.

To link a cell in one spreadsheet to a cell in another spreadsheet, first open both sheets. Move to the cell where you want the data to appear and enter: =

Now move to the cell from which the data will be linked. Press enter. The cell reference has been copied.

Each time you open a spreadsheet with a link the following message will be displayed.

Formatting and presenting your data

You should already know how to amend column widths to ensure data is displayed in full and how to display data using a variety of formats (such as integer, currency, and 2 decimal places).

Vertical and horizontal alignment, text orientation and wrap

To apply vertical and horizontal alignment, set text orientation and wrap cell contents:

To apply any of the formatting, you must first highlight the cells to which you want to apply that feature.

Click **Format, Cells, Alignment**.

Under **Text alignment**, you can specify your requirements for **Horizontal** and **Vertical** alignment.

Under **Text control** you can apply text wrap by clicking the **Wrap text** box.

Under **Text control** you can merge cells by clicking the **Merge cells** box. You must highlight all the cells you want to merge. You can then align the data – left, right or centred.

Sorting data

To sort data you must highlight the data, and all corresponding details.

Click **Data, Sort**.

Select the column on which you want to perform the sort. You can sort in ascending or descending order.

Format your page display and printing

You should already know how to print from a spreadsheet displaying either figures or formulae.

To change the **Orientation**, click **File, Page Setup** and **Page**. Select Portrait or Landscape.

To change the **Margins**, click **File, Page Setup** and **Margins**.

Make any changes you require.

To insert a Header and/or Footer, including the use of automatic fields (filename, page no, date), click **File, Page Setup** and **Header/Footer**.

You can then select either Custom Header or Custom Footer.

To enter automatic fields go to the position where you want the data to appear and click on the relevant icon.

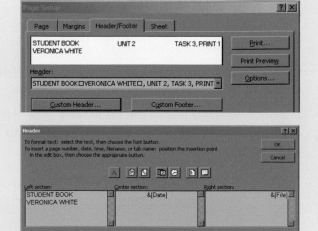

Gridlines and column and row headings – (A, B, C ...) and (I, 2, 3...)

From the spreadsheet file, click **File, Page Setup** and then the **Sheet tab**.

To print with gridlines click on the **Gridlines** box to enter the tick.

If the tick is not shown then the gridlines will not print.

To print with row and column headings click on the **Row and column headings** box to enter the tick.

If the tick is not shown then the row and column headings will not print.

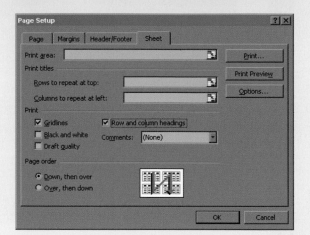

Cell borders

To apply cell borders go to the cell to which you want to apply the border. Select the border you want to apply and click on the icon.

Hide columns or rows

To hide columns or rows highlight the row(s) or column(s) you want to hide.

In this example rows 7 to 11 are to be hidden. Click **Format, Row, Hide**.

Build Up Exercises

TASK 1

This task is designed to allow you to practise some of the skills required to gain the OCR Level 2 Certificate for IT Users (CLAIT PLUS) assessment objectives for Unit 2 Spreadsheets. To cover all the assessment objectives you will have to complete Tasks 2 and 3.

Before you begin

You should know how to:

- enter, edit and manipulate data
- create formulae using absolute, relative and mixed references
- create formulae using common functions
- name a cell and use the named cell in a formula
- manage and print spreadsheet documents.

Scenario

You are working for an entertainment company that organises parties and shows for children. You are required to keep a record of the costs incurred when travelling to the shows and the amount spent on purchasing novelties for the parties.

The first file that you will update uses fixed costs for the packs purchased. You will have to complete the report using the specified data. You will provide details including the number of each novelty purchased, the costs of travel to the events, and totals for these items.

The company has decided to purchase a new vehicle, and you will provide some comparisons showing the expenses total depending on whether a diesel or petrol vehicle is purchased.

To produce the reports you will need the following file. You will find it on the CD provided with this book.

The data file, **runcost**, contains details of the costs and expenses.

TIP You might find it useful to look at this file before you begin the task to familiarise yourself with the data to be used.

You will need to refer to the:

- Formula Sheet

Your first task is to produce a report showing the year's costs and expenses to date. You will complete some of the formulae and print your work.

What You Have To Do

Assessment Objectives		
Ia, Ig	1	Open the data file **runcost** and save it in your software's normal file type. Use the filename **ytd1**.
3a	2	All the information needs to be visible. Amend all column widths to ensure that all the data is displayed in full.
3c, 3d	3	As an exception to the house style that you will be using later, in the **EXPENSES** and **COST BREAKDOWN** sections, set the text orientation for all the **column headings** to a +55 degree angle. Both horizontal and vertical alignment should be set to **centre**. They should be bold.
2c	4	In the **EXPENSES** section, adjacent to the text **Cost per mile**, name the cell (that contains the current value 0.34) **cpm**.
Ic, Id, Ie 2a, 2b	5	In the **COST DETAILS** section, refer to the Formula Sheet and generate the figures below for each of the novelties: **Pack cost** **Pack total**
Ic, Id, Ie 2a, 2c	6	In the **EXPENSE DETAILS** section, refer to the Formula Sheet and generate the figures below for each of the dates: **Cost per mile** **Total**
Ic, Ie	7	In the **EXPENSES** section, refer to the Formula Sheet and generate the figures below: **Expense Details Total** **Cost Details Total**
Ig	8	Save your work.
3a, 4a, 5a, 5b, 5c	9	Select an extract – from the **COST DETAILS** and **EXPENSE DETAILS** section headings down to the end of the spreadsheet.
		Using *only* one page, print this extract showing the figures. Make sure that all the data is displayed in full.
		Print in **landscape** orientation, and include **row** and **column headings**.
		Close your spreadsheet.

Before you begin

You should know how to:

- enter, edit and manipulate data
- create formulae and use common functions
- format and present data
- use spreadsheets to solve problems and project results
- print a specified selection of a spreadsheet to a stated number of pages.

Scenario

The company has decided to purchase a new vehicle, and you will provide some comparisons showing the expenses total depending on whether a diesel or petrol vehicle is purchased.

The second report uses data from the first task to update costings kept from previous years.

You will need to refer to the:

- House Style Sheet
- Formula Sheet

In this task you will amend data, complete the formulae using functions, format and print your work.

What You Have To Do	
Assessment Objectives	
	1 Open your file from Task 1 – **ytd1**.
1b, 1d, 3g	2 Make the following changes in the **Balloon packs section**.

2 (a) Some of the packs have been discontinued. Delete the rows for pack codes **B328** and **B329**.

(b) The codes are incorrect. Change them so that they all begin **BP** followed by the number – eg **BP292**.

(c) Some details have been omitted. Insert the data below, making sure that you copy any necessary formulae. You will also need to adjust the Cost Details Total to include the new data.

Novelty	Code	No of packs
Balloon packs	BP250	285
	BP455	200
	BP419	255
	BP210	290

(d) Sort the section so that the **codes** are in **ascending** order. Make sure that all the associated data is also sorted.

1c, 1e   3   In the **COST BREAKDOWN** section, using the functions SUM, COUNT or COUNTA, MIN, MAX and AVERAGE enter formulae to calculate for Toys, Gift packs and Balloon packs:
the number purchased
the number of different code types purchased
the minimum, maximum and average number purchased

What You Have To Do

Assessment Objectives		
Ib, If	4	It has been decided that a new vehicle must be purchased. To help with the decision of whether to buy a petrol or diesel vehicle, you are to provide some alternative figures. You will use the figures in the expenses section for diesel and petrol to provide these figures.

In the **EXPENSES** section:

(a) change the **Cost per mile** figure to **0.28**. The **Expense Details Total** figure will change. Enter this new figure in the cell next to the label **Diesel Total**.

(b) change the **Cost per mile** figure to **0.36**. The **Expense Details Total** figure will change. Enter this new figure in the cell next to the label **Petrol Total**.

Return the Cost per mile figure to the original value **0.34**.

Assessment Objectives		
Ig, 3b, 3c 3e, 3f, 4a 4b, 4c, 4d, 4e	5	You should apply the house style to your work, as detailed in the House Style Sheet, and then save your work.
3a, 5a, 5b	6	Select an extract – the **EXPENSES** section *only*. Using only one page, print this extract showing the figures. Make sure all the data is displayed in full.
5a, 5b, 5e	7	Select an extract – the **COST BREAKDOWN** section *only*. Using only one page, print this extract showing the formulae. Make sure all the data is displayed in full.
5a, 5b, 5e	8	Select an extract – the **EXPENSE DETAILS** section *only*. Using only one page, print this extract showing the formulae. Make sure all the data is displayed in full.
5a, 5b	9	Select an extract – the **COST DETAILS** section *only*. Using only one page, print this extract showing the figures. Make sure all the data is displayed in full.

TASK 3

Before you begin

You should know how to:

* link live data from one spreadsheet to another
* sort data
* manage and print spreadsheet documents.

To produce the reports you will need the following file:

Folder: **Unit 2**

Filename: **costings**

It contains details of the costs from previous years. You will find the file on the CD provided with this book.

TIP You might find it useful to look at this file before you begin the task to familiarise yourself with the data to be used.

You will need to refer to the:

- House Style Sheet
- Formula Sheet

Your next task will be to update a file containing on-going costings. You will link data to your first spreadsheet, complete an IF statement, hide columns, format and print your work.

What You Have To Do

Assessment Objectives		
Ia, Ig	1	Open the data file **costings** and save it in your software's normal file type. Use the filename **costs02**.
2d	2	In the **NOVELTIES** column, link the cell for **2002** to the **Cost Details Total** figure in the **ytd1** spreadsheet.
Ic, Id, Ie	3	Refer to the Formula Sheet and generate the **COSTINGS TOTAL** for each year.
Id, Ie	4	In the **DIFFERENCE** column, refer to the Formula Sheet and generate an IF statement to show the difference if the Parking Cost is more than 25% of the Mileage Cost for 1985. Replicate this formula for all the other years.
3b, 3c, 3e 3f, 4a, 4b 4c, 4d, 4e	5	You should apply the house style to the file, as detailed in the House Style Sheet.
3a, 5a, 5b	6	Using only one page, print your work showing the figures. Make sure that all the data is displayed. The orientation, margins, header and footer should be as specified in the House Style Sheet.
4f	7	Hide the columns from **NOVELTIES** to **COSTINGS TOTAL**.
5a, 5b, 5c, 5d, 5e	8	Using only one page, print your work showing the formulae (cell contents). Make sure that all the formulae are displayed in full and that the hidden columns are *not* printed. Display **gridlines** and **row** and **column** headings. The orientation, margins, header and footer should be as specified in the House Style Sheet.

House Style Sheet – Tasks 1 to 3

Page setup

- Use A4 paper
- Use landscape orientation
- Margins:
	top	2.5 cm
	bottom	2 cm
	left	2.5 cm
	right	1.5 cm
- Header: candidate name
- Footer: automatic date field (English format, eg dd/mm/yy), page number and filename

Text style

Feature	Font	Font size	Style	Alignment
Main title	serif	16	bold, capitals framed by box	centred across all columns that contain data
Section headings	sans serif	11	bold, capitals framed by box	centred across the columns making up the section
Column headings	sans serif	10	bold	horizontal: centre vertical: centre apply text wrap
Body	sans serif	10	no emphasis	left unless otherwise stated

The section headings in this assignment are:
EXPENSES
COST BREAKDOWN
COST DETAILS
EXPENSE DETAILS

Number style

Feature	Font	Font size	Style	Alignment
Monetary amounts	sans serif	10	2 decimal places – do not show monetary symbols unless specified	right
Date	sans serif	10	English format (dd/mm/yy)	right
Other numbers	sans serif	10	0 decimal places unless otherwise stated	right unless otherwise stated

Formula Sheet – Tasks I to 3

To complete the tasks you will need to use a variety of different cell references (relative, absolute, mixed and named cell) in the formulae. The following information has been provided to help you with your tasks.

Pack cost	Enter the formulae using the relevant **Cost** figures for Toys, Gift packs and Balloon packs in the EXPENSES section. You may use absolute or mixed cell referencing.
Pack total	Multiply the No of packs by the Pack cost.
Cost per mile	Use the named cell – **cpm**.
Total	Multiply the Cost per mile by the Mileage figure.
Expense Details Total	Add together all the figures in the Total column of the EXPENSE DETAILS section.
Cost Details Total	Add together all the figures in the Pack total column of the COST DETAILS section.
COSTINGS TOTAL	Add together the figures for NOVELTIES, PARKING and MILEAGE COST.
DIFFERENCE	Use an IF statement to display the difference if the PARKING cost is more than 25% of the MILEAGE COST.

UNIT 3 Databases

This unit is designed to test your ability to use database software to create a simple file from source documents. You will also use another file, which you will amend. You will carry out searches, then sort and format the results to provide reports.

You may find it easier to undertake this unit if you have completed the Databases unit at Level 1. If you have done so, you will already know how to:

- identify and use database software correctly
- use an input device to enter and edit data accurately
- create simple queries/searches on one or two criteria
- present selected data sorted alphabetically, numerically and by date
- manage and print database files.

To pass this unit

You must complete the three-hour OCR-set assignment without making any critical errors, and with no more than three accuracy errors. If you do not achieve a Pass you may re-take the assessment using a different assignment.

You cannot claim more than one unit from the same application area towards the 3 optional units of the Level 2 qualification, due to an overlap in content – ie you may choose one from Unit 3 Databases, Unit 11 Databases Solutions or Unit 19 Databases (Microsoft Office Specialist Access Core).

Your work will be marked by your tutor, and externally moderated by OCR.

Critical errors

- Errors in entering numeric data that could be used in calculations.
- Missing title, or field headings on any printout.
- Incorrect search results.

- Produces incorrect numeric values on reports/queries.
- Produces incorrect sort order.
- Any missing field in reports, queries or labels.

Accuracy errors

- Each instance of an error in entering data. In this unit apply one data entry error for any error(s) in a field, a title, or a field heading.
- Each instance of an error in completing an assessment objective.

What will you learn?

When you have completed this unit you should be able to:

- create a database file, set up fields and enter test data
- import and interrogate data using complex search criteria
- present data in various report formats including list and labels
- format and present reports.

How to meet the assessment objectives

You will be introduced to **one** method of achieving the assessment objectives. There will be other methods of carrying out these tasks. Only objectives that were not covered in Level 1 are included.

You will already know how to enter and edit data, create simple queries, sort, manage and print database files.

Now we will deal with the new areas.

Creating and saving a database

Open the program Access.

Click on **Blank Access database** then click **OK**.

Enter the name of your database.

Set up field names

Enter the **Field Name**, for example Company Name.

Set up data types for fields

Click on the down arrow in the **Data Type** box.

Select the appropriate type from the options given.

Repeat this for all the fields you wish to enter.

Select **Create table in Design view**.

Click on **Create**.

Click on ▨

Set appropriate field lengths

From the **General** tab, click in the **Field Size** box then enter the appropriate size.

For numeric fields, click on the down arrow at the end of the **Format** box then select the appropriate display.

Save table/query/report

Click on 💾

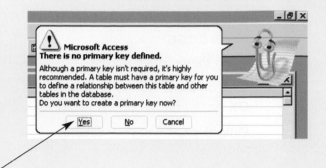

Enter the name of your table/query/report.

Click **OK**.

Access will prompt you to add a primary key.

A primary key uniquely identifies each record stored in a table. It is always best to have a primary key.

Click on **Yes** then close the window.

Click on the appropriate icon from the **Objects** menu to view the tables, queries or reports you have created.

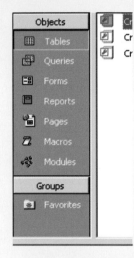

Format reports

Select **Reports** from the **Objects** menu.

Click on 🔳 **New**

Select the type of report you require.

For most purposes it is best to use the Report Wizard.

Click on the down arrow to select the table/query on which your report is to be based.

Click **OK**.

In **Available Fields** click on field(s) to be included.

Click on ⟩ to move to **Selected Fields**.

The wizard will take you through a series of steps. These steps allow you to specify how you want the data in the report to be displayed.

Select: **Grouping**　　　**Sorting**　　　　　**Display**　　　　　**Style**

Click on **Finish**.

Insert the title of the report.

Click on **Finish**.

You will be presented with a preview of the report.

You will probably need to insert headers or footers, and you may need to make adjustments to your report. These amendments are made in Design view.

Insert automatic headers/footers (filename, page number, date)

From any report click on ![Design] Design

Select the text box containing the **Page Header** or **Page Footer**.

Use the **toolbar** to change the **alignment**, **font size** and **style** of the text.

Toolbar

In Design view, any items can be moved and formatted

Footer can be changed, moved and formatted

With the text box selected you can move page items to the required position by holding and dragging to the new location. A hand will appear as you drag the item.

Note: **Report Header** appears only on the first page and **Report Footer** only on the last page.

Access normally inserts page numbers and the date automatically.

To insert automatic date and page numbers click on the **Insert Menu**, select **Page Numbers** and/or **Date and Time**. Select the display from the options listed.

To create a new text header or footer manually (eg to insert your name), click on the **Label** icon **Aa**. Draw a text box in the header/footer area. Enter the required text.

Other information may be entered using the **Text Box** icon **ab**.

Entering: **=Now()** inserts the current date and time.
="Page"&[Page] inserts page numbers.
=[Caption] inserts the **filename**.

Note: Access will automatically insert a second text box showing the text number. This can be amended to include a description of the function or can be deleted to prevent it showing on the report.

To change headers/footers automatically

Select the box containing the header/footer.

Click on the **right** mouse button, select **Properties**.

From the **Data tab** click in the **Control Source** box, press **delete** to remove the current entry.

Click on ...

Enter **=** in the top box.

Click on **Common Expressions** in the first column.

In the second column you can select the entry (eg Page number or Date).

Select **Paste**, **OK**.

Close the window.

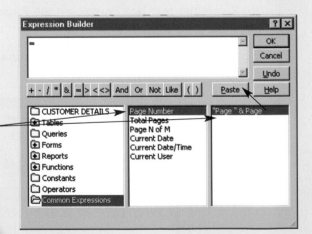

To insert the filename follow the steps from:
Select the box …
to
Enter **=** in the top box

Select the file (usually the first folder), then select **Caption** in the third column, click on **Paste**, **OK** then close the window.

To **delete** a header/footer, click on the header/footer then press the **Delete** key.

Insert group headers

Group headers can be inserted using the Report Wizard. You can also add these in Design view by clicking on the **Sorting and Grouping** icon

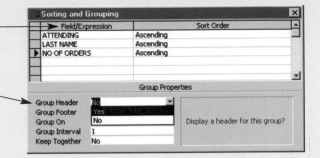

In the **Field/Expression** column, click at the end of the first box, then select the field for your group heading and the sort order.

In **Group Properties**, click at the end on the **Group Header** box, select **Yes**.

Close the window.

Import and interrogate database

Import/open data file

To open a generic file (such as a csv file) in **Access**, open a new database file.

Select **File** then **Get External Data**.

Click on **Import**. Locate and select the file.

Note: in the **Files of type** box you must select **Text Files**.

Access will present you with options regarding the data and how it is going to import it. If your data contains field names, at Step 2, click in the box **First Row Contains Field Names**.

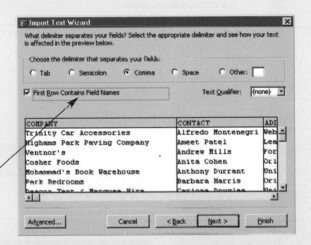

If your data does not include field names you will need to **enter** the **field names** and select **data types** at Step 4.

Add/amend/delete/records/fields

Most of these skills were covered in Level 1.

At Level 2 you will be working with much larger databases. To find records to amend/delete it is far more efficient to use the 'find' feature of the program.

If you only wish to find data in one particular field, click in that field before performing the find.

From the **Edit** menu select **Find** or use the find icon.

Select **Find** or **Replace**.

Key in the words you wish to find/replace.

Click in the **Look in** box to select the whole table or a selected field.

You can also select where in the field to search by clicking at the end of the **Match** box.

The options given are **Whole Field, Any Part of Field** or **Start of Field** (useful if you want to replace the start of a code but not the end of it, eg **xx**1234xx could be replaced with **ds**1234xx.)

The **xx** at the end of the code would not be replaced.

Clicking on the **More** button allows you to select to match the case and/or search **Up, Down** or **All** the database.

Use logical operators in queries

A logical field is a field in which the data is either Yes or No (True or False). In Access, data entered in logical fields is usually displayed using a tick box. The box contains a tick if the entry is "Yes" and is blank if the entry is "No".

Tick to show field

You may try this section using the **sample** database on the CD that accompanies this book.

Select **Queries** from the **Objects** menu then click on the **New** icon.

Select **Design view**,

Select the **table** or **query** on which you want your query to be based.

Click on **Add** then close the window.

Note: If you add the item twice it will duplicate the information!

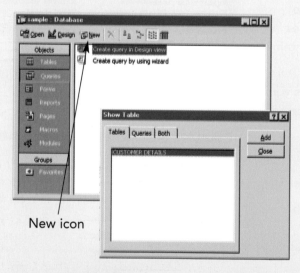

New icon

Click in the first **Field** box, click on the down arrow, select the field you want to appear first in your query.

Repeat for all fields you wish to display and/or query.

The order in which you select fields will be the way the fields are displayed for the query.

In the column with the field that contains the data you wish to query, click in the **Criteria** box and enter your query.

You may query any number of fields.

When querying a logical field the **Criteria** would be either **Yes** or **No**. (The logical fields in the sample database are MODEL and ATTENDING). Check that a tick appears in the **Show** box of all the fields you wish to print.

Save and close the query.

Use range operators in queries

You can create a query to select records within a specified range.

Example

All people born after 1980 and before 1995.

Enter **>1980 And <1995** (more than 1980 and less than 1995).

To include those people born in 1980 and 1995 = needs to be added.

Enter **>=1980 And <=1995**.

For only those people born in 1980 and also those people born in 1995.

Enter **=1980 Or =1995**.

Using **And** would have returned no results, a person could not have been born in 1980 and 1995!

Calculated fields take information from two or more fields and calculate the result.

Example

To calculate

Pay by multiplying the *Hours* by the *Rate*

In Design view select the fields you wish to show.

In a blank field enter **Pay: [Hours]*[Rate]**.

The pay will be calculated and shown in the *Pay* field.

Combine search criteria using logical operators

You can create a query based on several different criteria.

Example

Those *BORN* between 1980 and 1995 *and* who are *ATTENDING*.

The criteria for *BORN* would be **>=1980 And <=1995** *and* the criteria for *ATTENDING* would be **Yes**.

Another common search is the **OR** query. You might want to find all *FEMALES*, and only the *MALES* who live in Walthamstow.

This would be entered as shown below:

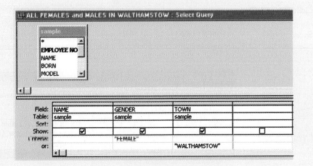

A wild card * can be used in queries when searching.

Example

To search for product codes PR234, PR231, PR876 etc.

Enter the criteria **Like "PR*"** to find PR anywhere in the code. We would enter **Like "*PR*"** the * representing anything.

You will need to know the following mathematical operators:

> more than	**<= less than or**
= equal to	**equal to**
< less than	**>= more than or**
<> not equal to	**equal to**

Data displayed in full

Check your printouts very carefully. Pay particular attention to headings.

Reports can be adjusted in **Design** view, queries can be adjusted in the open query.

Always check in print preview before printing.

Data presented in a specified order

The fields in your query are presented in the order you have selected the **Fields** in Design view.

Select to sort by clicking in the **Sort** cell of the field you wish to arrange.

You may sort in **ascending** (A–Z) or (1–100) or in **descending** order (Z–A) or (100–1). The example below will show *BORN* and *ATTENDING* in that order.

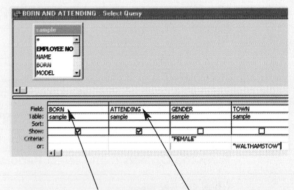

Only fields *BORN* and *ATTENDING* will be shown.

In Reports, Step 4 of the Report Wizard allows you to specify fields to be sorted and the sort order. The field on which you have performed the sort will appear first in your report.

Use search results to produce a report

'Search results' are usually referred to as queries.

To produce a report using a query, specify the name of the query at Step 1 of the Report Wizard.

Data is presented in a table/list format

When you open a query the data is displayed in a table/list format.

In a report the **Report Wizard** enables you to select a Tabular display at Step 5.

Data is presented in group format

In a report the **Report Wizard** enables you to group on up to 4 levels at Step 3.

Data is presented in record/columnar format for label printing

From the **Objects** menu select **Reports**.

Click on 📄 New

Select **Label Wizard**.

Select your options from each menu.

You may use the **back** button to amend mistakes.

If you wish to display several fields on one line, press the space bar after you have added each field.

The wizard allows you to perform several levels of sort (eg, first by Surname, then by Post Code).

To adjust your margins to print your labels/reports or queries on the specified number of page(s), click on the **File** menu then select **Page Setup**.

You can adjust:

- the margins
- select to print the data only
- page orientation (landscape/portrait)
- columns (number, row spacing, height and width).

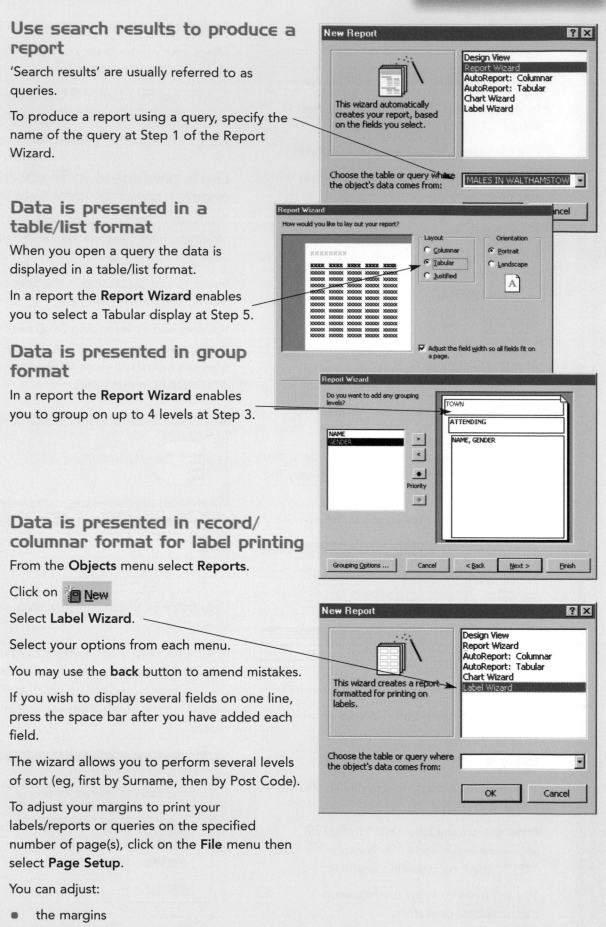

Display summaries

The sort step of the **Report Wizard** gives you an option to produce a group summary.

Click on the **Summary Options** button to select the summary you require. The summary will then be included in the report.

Using this function may give you more information than you require, or may not give you the information you want.

Adjust the report in the Design view once your report has been generated. Shown below is part of the output of the report.

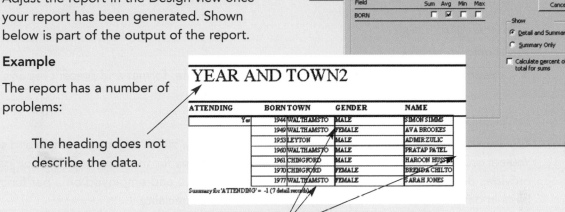

Example

The report has a number of problems:

The heading does not describe the data.

Not all the information is visible. Summary for ATTENDING is not required. I would like to COUNT the number attending instead.

The adjustments need to be made in Design view.

Before:

After:

Heading amended

Text amended to add clarity   Summary detail removed   Count function and label added

All labels adjusted and/or moved and aligned

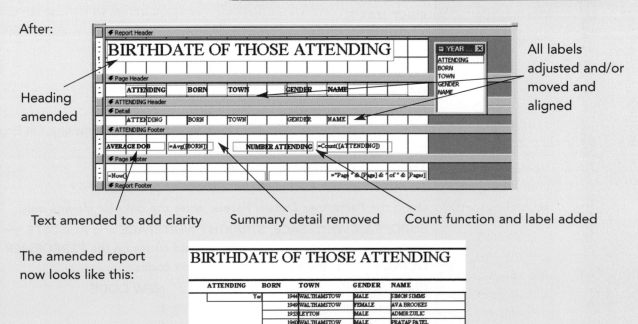

The amended report now looks like this:

Build Up Exercises

TASK

1

This task is designed to allow you to practise some of the skills required to gain the OCR Level 2 Certificate for IT Users (CLAIT PLUS) assessment objectives for Unit 3 Databases. To cover all the assessment objectives you will have to complete Tasks 2 and 3.

Before you begin

You should know how to:

● create a database file; set up fields and enter test data; format and present reports.

Scenario

You are working for an entertainment company, Creativity, which organises parties and shows. You are responsible for creating and maintaining databases for the company. The company provides different types of clown. The clowns are freelance and employed on a per function basis in different parts of the country. Each clown has a speciality.

What You Have To Do

Assessment Objectives		
1a, 1b, 1c, 1d	1	**You need to set up a database of clowns who have worked for the company.** Open your database software and create a new database called **CLOWNS**. Create a table called **DETAILS** using the following field headings. You should use field sizes and types (eg text, numeric, date, yes/no) appropriate to the data.

You need to set up a database of clowns who have worked for the company.

Open your database software and create a new database called **CLOWNS**. Create a table called **DETAILS** using the following field headings. You should use field sizes and types (eg text, numeric, date, yes/no) appropriate to the data.

FIELD HEADING	
SURNAME	
FIRST NAME	
ADDRESS	
TOWN	
COUNTY	
DAYS	
FEE	currency, 2 decimal places
LAST DATE	the last date the clown worked for the company – in English format (eg dd/mm/yy)
TYPE	use code (E, S or A)
TRAVELS	use a Y/N field for TRAVELS OUT OF TOWN

1e   2 Using the **Performer Details Forms**, enter the data for **clowns only**.

EUROPEAN WHITEFACE, STRAIGHT WHITEFACE and **AUGUSTE** are types of clown. They are shown by the old codes on the **PERFORMER DETAILS** forms. You should enter the **new** codes:

CLOWN TYPE	OLD CODE	NEW CODE
European Whiteface	EUR	E
Straight Whiteface	STR	S
Auguste	AUG	A

Performer Details Forms

FIRST NAME	Tony	INITIALS	C. G.
SURNAME	Thomas	TEL NO.	628 1922
ADDRESS	9 Mason Crescent	TOWN	York
COUNTY	North Yorks	FEE	£85
DAYS	120	LAST DATE	23/10/01
CLOWN	Yes	CLOWN TYPE	EUR
TRAVELS OUT OF TOWN	No		

FIRST NAME	Alan	INITIALS	J.
SURNAME	Chambers	TEL NO.	663 1099
ADDRESS	42 Bond Road	TOWN	Margate
COUNTY	Kent	FEE	£107.50
DAYS	67	LAST DATE	6/1/02
CLOWN	Yes	CLOWN TYPE	AUG
TRAVELS OUT OF TOWN	Yes		

FIRST NAME	Thore	INITIALS	A.
SURNAME	Stein	TEL NO.	555 1212
ADDRESS	7 Linty Street	TOWN	Kendal
COUNTY	Cumbria	FEE	£95
DAYS	23	LAST DATE	20/2/02
CLOWN	Yes	CLOWN TYPE	STR
TRAVELS OUT OF TOWN	Yes		

FIRST NAME	Michael	INITIALS	L.
SURNAME	Bisok	TEL NO.	267 9121
ADDRESS	4 Bedford Place	TOWN	Carlisle
COUNTY	Cumbria	FEE	£65
DAYS	4	LAST DATE	1/3/02
CLOWN	Yes	CLOWN TYPE	EUR
TRAVELS OUT OF TOWN	No		

FIRST NAME	Nadine	INITIALS	K
SURNAME	Henschel	TEL NO.	481 6658
ADDRESS	30 Binbrook Road	TOWN	York
COUNTY	North Yorks	FEE	£99
DAYS	95	LAST DATE	24/04/02
CLOWN	Yes	CLOWN TYPE	EUR
TRAVELS OUT OF TOWN	Yes		

Performer Details Forms

FIRST NAME	Joao	INITIALS	C.
SURNAME	Veloso	TEL NO.	346 8315
ADDRESS	9 Falcon Road	TOWN	Hastings
COUNTY	Kent	FEE	£105
DAYS	89	LAST DATE	23/3/02
CLOWN	Yes	CLOWN TYPE	AUG
TRAVELS OUT OF TOWN		No	

FIRST NAME	Jason	INITIALS	R.
SURNAME	Cartwright	TEL NO.	655 8613
ADDRESS	31 Forest Road	TOWN	Hastings
COUNTY	Kent	FEE	£75
DAYS	72	LAST DATE	18/2/02
CLOWN	Yes	CLOWN TYPE	STR
TRAVELS OUT OF TOWN		Yes	

FIRST NAME	Robert	INITIALS	N.H.
SURNAME	Wallace	TEL NO.	474 1115
ADDRESS	3 Ludlow Court	TOWN	Carlisle
COUNTY	Cumbria	FEE	£250
DAYS	6	LAST DATE	24/12/01
CLOWN	No	CLOWN TYPE	
TRAVELS OUT OF TOWN		No	

FIRST NAME	Michael	INITIALS	S.
SURNAME	Murphy	TEL NO.	501 6300
ADDRESS	2 Hawthorne Road	TOWN	Margate
COUNTY	Kent	FEE	£95.50
DAYS	47	LAST DATE	20/02/02
CLOWN	Yes	CLOWN TYPE	AUG
TRAVELS OUT OF TOWN		Yes	

FIRST NAME	Julian	INITIALS	G.L.S.
SURNAME	Northam	TEL NO.	491 3803
ADDRESS	16 Weaford Lane	TOWN	Kendal
COUNTY	Cumbria	FEE	£175
DAYS	0	LAST DATE	
CLOWN	No	CLOWN TYPE	
TRAVELS OUT OF TOWN		Yes	

Performer Details Forms

FIRST NAME	Denise	INITIALS	
SURNAME	Hart	TEL NO.	212 9086
ADDRESS	34 Topcliffe Drive	TOWN	Thirsk
COUNTY	North Yorks	FEE	£105
DAYS	28	LAST DATE	20/12/01
CLOWN	Yes	CLOWN TYPE	EUR
TRAVELS OUT OF TOWN		No	

FIRST NAME	Wayne	INITIALS	K
SURNAME	Hislop	TEL NO.	455 0976
ADDRESS	9 Lime Avenue	TOWN	Louth
COUNTY	Lincolnshire	FEE	£150
DAYS	0	LAST DATE	
CLOWN	No	CLOWN TYPE	
TRAVELS OUT OF TOWN		Yes	

FIRST NAME	Jennifer	INITIALS	B.C.
SURNAME	Mercer	TEL NO.	656 1892
ADDRESS	2 Ripon Way	TOWN	Penrith
COUNTY	Cumbria	FEE	£95
DAYS	129	LAST DATE	29/3/02
CLOWN	Yes	CLOWN TYPE	STR
TRAVELS OUT OF TOWN		No	

What You Have To Do

Assessment Objectives		
If	3	Save your table, retaining the name **DETAILS**.
2a, 2b, 2d, 2e, 4a, 4b, 4c, 4e	4	You have to produce a report. Your manager wants the information in a tabular format.
		Present the fields in the order given in step 1. Do *not* include the **COUNTY** field. Ensure that all data is displayed in full.
		Sort the data in ascending order of **LAST DATE**.
		Give the report the title: **PERFORMER DETAILS**
		Insert today's date (as an automatic field), your name and centre number in a **footer**.
		Print the report in **landscape** orientation.
If	5	Save your report as DETREP.

TASK 2

Before you begin

You should know how to:

- insert a field
- present data in various report formats including list and labels
- format and present reports
- You have been asked to provide some reports from the file you have set up.

What You Have To Do

Assessment Objectives		
1f, 3b, 3f	1	You have been asked to provide a report showing the amount paid to each clown by the company. You will have to enter a new field and carry out a calculation in that field to provide the report.
		Add a new field named **PAYMENTS** to the **DETAILS** table. Set the field type to **CURRENCY, 2 decimal places**.
		The value can be calculated by multiplying **DAYS** by **FEE**.
		Save your amended table.
1f, 2a, 2b, 2e, 4b, 4c	2	Prepare your report with the fields:
		FIRST NAME, SURNAME, TOWN, DAYS, FEE, PAYMENTS
		Sort the data in ascending order of **SURNAME**.
		Give the report the title: **PAYMENTS**
		Add your name and centre number in a **footer**.
		Save the report as **PAYMENTS**.
2a, 4a, 4e	3	Print the **PAYMENTS** report on one page, in tabular format, **portrait** orientation.
		Ensure that all field headings, records and your name are fully displayed.
2a, 4a, 4b, 4c, 4g	4	You have been asked to produce name tags for the annual meeting. Create labels from the **DETAILS** table and display information from the following fields (field names should not be included on the labels).
		FIRST NAME SURNAME (on one line) **TOWN** **TYPE**
		Sort the labels by **TOWN** and then by **SURNAME**.
		Ensure that the data on row one is separated by at least one space.
		Print the labels on one page ensuring that each name is fully displayed.

TASK 3

In this task you will use the data file **cusfile**. You will find the file on the CD that accompanies this book. The file content is shown below – there should be 100 records. This task will allow you to practise working with a large data file. When you carry out your assessment you will be provided with a file from OCR. The OCR file will also contain about 100 records.

Scenario

The company keeps a customer database showing those customers for whom the company has presented events. You have been asked to interrogate the file to produce information in preparation for the forthcoming annual meeting, and in response to queries. You will change details on the file and interrogate it to produce queries and reports.

The field headings, types and formats in **cusfile** are:

Field name	Field type	Format
SURNAME	Text	
FIRST NAME	Text	
NO	Number	Integer
STREET	Text	
TOWN	Text	
COUNTY	Text	
SEX	M/F	M or F
DOB	Date/Time	dd/mmm/yy
ACT	Text	E or S or A

What You Have To Do

Assessment Objectives		
Ia, Ib, If, 3a, 4a	I	Import the data file **cusfile** and save it in your software's normal file type. Check that the field names are correct. Make sure that the field type and format is correct. Ensure that all the information is fully displayed.
3b	2	Ken Voss has asked to be removed from the company database. Delete his record.
3b	3	Add these new customers:

Details	New customer 1	New customer 2
SURNAME	HERGES	LAKSHMI
FIRST NAME	KIMBERLEY	JAYA
NO	51	34
STREET	WOOD STREET	WINTON AVENUE
TOWN	KENDAL	WORKINGTON
COUNTY	CUMBRIA	CUMBRIA
SEX	F	M
DOB	5/1/36	31/7/38
ACT	A	S

What You Have To Do

Assessment Objectives		
3b	4	We have found out that some of the customer information is incorrect. Change this information:

- GERARD **HOUSEMAN** has been entered incorrectly as GERARD HOUSER
- DOB for PATRICIA **HALE** should be **03/11/35**
- ANNE MOORE lives at **48** HAMLET WAY
- BELINDA DEJONG lives at **7** ASHGROVE ROAD

If, 3d	5	The company has introduced a new act designed for senior citizens, and wants to inform suitable contacts. You have been asked to provide the details.

Create a query to find all customers born **before 01/01/43**. Save this query as **GOLDEN**.

If, 2a, 2b, 2d, 2e, 4a, 4b, 4c, 4d, 4e	6	Use the **GOLDEN** query to produce a TABULAR REPORT. Print using **landscape** orientation. Adjust the margins to ensure that your printout fits on one page.

Display the fields in this order:

COUNTY, SURNAME, FIRST NAME, NO, STREET, TOWN, DOB

Sort the data in ascending order of **COUNTY**.

Give the report the title: **GOLDEN CLUB**

Use *only* the date, your name and centre number in the footer.

Save the report as **GCLUB**.

Ensure that **all** the data is fully displayed, and print.

If, 3c	7	The company has been approached by a new act – a duo. They live in Deal, but would be prepared to work in Margate as well. One of the performers is a European Whiteface clown, the other an Auguste. They want to know what business you do in the area.

Provide a new query showing all customers living in Margate or Deal who have used either clown type. Save the query as **KENT**.

If, 2a, 2b, 2c, 2d, 2e, 4a, 4b, 4c, 4d, 4f	8	Produce a report based on the query **KENT**. Print the report in a tabular format, using **portrait** orientation.

Print these fields only:	**SURNAME, FIRST NAME, TOWN, ACT**
Group the report by:	**TOWN** and **ACT**
Sort on:	**SURNAME** (ascending order)
Give the report the title:	**KENT CLOWN BOOKINGS**

Use an automatic field for the date, and add your name and centre number in the footer (right aligned).

Save the report as **KENTCLOW**.

Ensure that **all** the data is fully displayed. Adjust the margins to fit on one page only, and print.

What You Have To Do

If, 2a, 2b, 2d, 3e, 4a 4b, 4c, 4e

9 A festival of Auguste clowns is to be held. One of the workshops will involve the application of the typical Auguste makeup. Some of the customers who were introduced to face painting at events have expressed an interest and it has been decided that the company will target all female customers who have already booked an Auguste act. You have been asked to provide the details.

Produce a new query to show the details for these customers. Save the query as **AUGUSTE**.

Display the fields in this order:
SURNAME, FIRST NAME, TOWN, COUNTY, SEX, ACT

Sort the data in ascending order of **COUNTY**.

The filename and date should appear in the header, the automatic page number in the footer.

Print the query in a tabular format in **portrait** orientation.

Ensure that **all** the data is fully displayed. Ensure your printout fits onto one page, and print.

If, 3e

10 Having looked at the list, it has been decided to restrict the potential participants to customers in Cumbria, Lancashire and Merseyside.

Amend the query to exclude customers in any other county. Do not make any other changes to the query.

Save the query as **AUGPP**.

2a, 2b, 2c, 2e, 4a, 4b, 4c, 4d, 4f 4h

11 Use the query **AUGPP** to produce a tabular report. Print on one page in **portrait** orientation.

Display these fields only: **SURNAME, FIRST NAME, TOWN, COUNTY**

Group by **COUNTY** and **TOWN**.

Sort the data in ascending order of **SURNAME**.

Count the number in each county. Display the figure at the end of the County heading line in each section. Give the count figure the label: **County Total**

Give the report the title: **AUGUSTE MAKEUP WORKSHOP**

Display *only* your name and centre number in the footer.

Make sure that **all** the data is fully displayed.

Save as AMW, and print.

UNIT 4 Desktop Publishing

This unit is designed to test your ability to use desktop publishing software to create a publication. You will work from a design brief.

You may find it easier to undertake this unit if you have completed the Desktop Publishing unit at Level 1. If you have done so, you will already know how to:

- identify and use appropriate software correctly
- set up a standard page layout and text properties
- import and place text and image files
- manipulate text and images to balance page
- manage publications and print composite proofs.

To pass this unit

You must complete the three-hour OCR-set assignment without making any critical errors, and with no more than three accuracy errors. If you do not achieve a Pass you may re-take the assessment using a different assignment.

You cannot claim both Unit 4 Desktop Publishing and Unit 12 Desktop Publishing Solutions towards the three optional units of the Level 2 qualification, due to an overlap in content.

Your work will be marked by your tutor, and externally moderated by OCR.

Critical errors

- Any specified text file is missing.
- Any specified text file is incomplete.
- A specified image is missing.
- Failure to print colour-separated copies.

Accuracy errors

- Each instance of an error in entering data. In this unit apply one data entry error for any error(s) in each word. **Note:** the imported text is not assessed for accuracy.
- Each instance of an error in completing an assessment objective.

What will you learn?

When you have completed this unit you should be able to:

- set up a master page and style sheet according to a design brief
- import and manipulate text and image file(s)
- amend publication content using proof correction symbols
- prepare a publication for press.

How to meet the assessment objectives

You will be introduced to **one** method of achieving the assessment objectives. There will be other methods of carrying out these tasks. Only objectives that were not covered in Level 1 are included.

You will already know how to set up a standard page layout and text properties, import and place text and image files, copyfit, manage publications and print composite proofs.

Now we will deal with the new areas.

Setting up a master page and style sheet from a design brief

Setting the document size

From the **Tools** menu, select **Options**, **General**, enter the **Start** page number.

Set the **Measurement units**.

Click on **OK**.

From the **File** menu, select **Page Setup**.

Click in **Special Size**.

Enter the **Width** and **Height**.

Select the **Orientation**.

Click on **OK**.

To insert pages click on **Insert**, **Page**.

Enter **Number of new pages**.

Select how you want your pages to be set up.

To set up your master page click on **View**, select **Go to Background**.

The items on the master page will be displayed on every page of your document.

Setting margins

From the **Arrange** menu, select **Layout Guides**.

Enter the margins.

Enter the columns.

Click on **OK**.

Setting up headers and footers

From the **View menu**, select **Go to Background**.

Use the text tool [A] to draw a text box.

Enter the header or footer.

Move the text box to the position required.

The text box has default margins of 0.1 cm all round.

To line up your text with the margin, click **Format**, **Text Frame Properties**, change the margin(s) to 0 cm.

If you have aligned your text box, your header or footer will now be positioned in line with the margin.

To enter page numbers and automatic date into your header, click **Insert**, **Date and Time** or **Page Numbers**.

To start at a page number other than 1, click on **Tools**, go to **Options**, then **General**. Enter the start page number.

Creating columns

To set 'background' columns see above under setting margins.

You can also set up columns in text frames. See below.

Creating text frames

Study the Page layout diagram for your publication **very carefully**. Using the text frame tool **A** draw the required text frames to suit your publication.

Text frames will have a white background. To make text frames transparent (to see your layout guides) select the text frame, press **Ctrl+T**. Pressing Ctrl+T again restores the white background.

Setting gutter space according to a design brief

Columns can be set up within a text frame. From **View** select **Go to Foreground**.

Draw a text box to the exact size of the pink margin guides.

Click on **Format**, select **Text Frame Properties**.

Change all margins to 0 cm.

Select the **Number** of columns.

Select the **Spacing** between columns.

Selecting **Wrap text around objects** allows you to create multiple frame layouts on one page.

Here is an example.

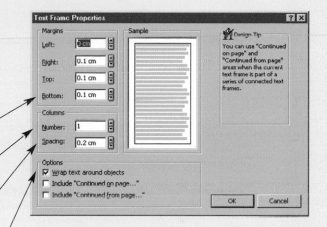

| The text continues in the first column flowing around the first part of the text. It then flows to the 2nd and 3rd columns of the page. | In this story the text starts in a text frame that has been drawn across several of the columns in the centre of the page.

You may have as many text frames on the page as you wish. | Notice that the top text frame has been left with a white background. The background of the large text frame has been set to transparent. |

Setting up style sheets

Click on **Format, Text Style**.

Click on **Create a new style**.

Enter the name of the style (eg Body Text).

Click on **Character type and size** to set these items, then click **OK**.

Bullets can be added here.

When you have completed your style click **OK**.

To create your next style click on Normal. Repeat from **Create a new style** for each of your text styles.

When you have created all your text styles click on **Close**.

Saving your master page

Click on 💾

Select **Publisher Template**.

Click **Save**.

Importing and manipulating text and image files

Importing a text file

Click your mouse in the position you want the text to start.

Click on **Insert**, **Text File**.

Select the file you wish to insert.

Text will fill the frame, extra text will be indicated by **A•••**

To flow the text into another frame click on **A•••** from the toolbar, click on the link icon to link your text.

You will now see the jug icon

Position the jug where you want the text to flow and click.

The arrow indicates the direction of the text flow.

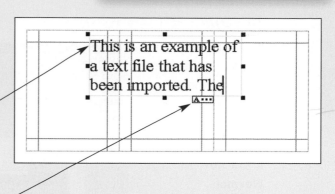

Importing an image file

Click on **Insert**, **Picture.**

Select the image and click on **Insert**.

You may need to adjust the size of the image.

Click on **Format**, **Scale Picture.**

Adjust the **Scale height** and **Scale width** to the same % to keep it in proportion.

In the example opposite the image has been scaled to 10%.

Placing content according to text flow diagrams and a design brief

Study the design brief *very carefully*. Text will not necessarily start in the first column or on the first page of your document.

Applying styles to text

To apply body text to your entire story click anywhere in the text and press **Ctrl+A**.

Click on the down arrow next to **Normal**.

Click on **body text**.

Apply the other styles by clicking on the appropriate text in your publication.

Click on the down arrow next to **Normal**.

Click on the style you wish to apply.

This example shows styles applied.

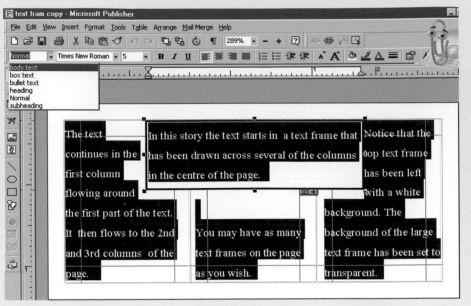

Headline →
Body Text →
Box Text →
Subheading →

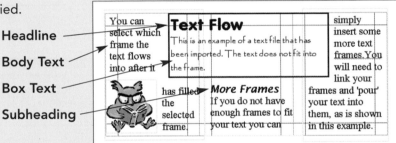

Layering graphics and text

Select the text frame.

Click on **Format, Text Frame Properties**.

Click on **Wrap text around objects** to remove the tick.

70

Select the graphic then press **Shift+F6** to send it to the background.

Select the text frame, then re-set the **Text Frame Properties** to **Wrap text around objects** to restore wrap around other frames.

Inserting and formatting lines and boxes

You can draw lines and boxes to the exact size you require by using the drawing tools on the toolbar.

Hold down the Shift key while you are drawing to keep the line straight or to make the box perfectly square.

To insert a box around a frame select the frame.

Click **Format, Line/Border Style**.

Select the line you require.

To customise the style click on the line/border.

Click **Format**.

Select **Line/Border Style**.

Then **More**.

Click on **BorderArt**.

Select the style you require.

Click on **Apply**.

Creating reverse text on solid or shaded backgrounds

Highlight the text. On the toolbar click on the **Font Colour** icon, select white. With the text still selected click on the **Fill Colour** icon and fill with black or the solid colour required. To shade the box click on the **Font Colour** icon, click **Fill Effects**. Click in the shade panel showing the shade you require, click **Apply** then close the window.

Rotating text or objects

Select the text frame or object to be rotated. From the **Arrange** menu, select **Rotate or Flip**. **Rotate Left** rotates 90° to the left, **Rotate Right** rotates 90° to the right. Selecting **Custom Rotate** allows you to enter the precise angle for the rotation. Enter the angle, click on **Apply** then **Close**.

Applying dropped capitals

Select the capital to be dropped.

Click on **Format, Drop Cap**.

Click on **Custom Drop Cap**.

Select **Size of letters** and choose number of lines you want the letter to drop.

Click on **Apply**.

Amending publication content

Cropping an image

Use ⊹ to crop images.

To crop from the left, position the cropping tool as shown.

Holding down on the mouse, slide to remove the part of the image you do not require.

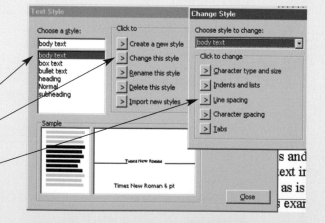

Amending leading

In Publisher **leading** is controlled by **Line spacing**. The default is 1sp. You can adjust the leading precisely by adding 2 digits after the decimal point, for example 1.15, 1.31 etc.

To keep leading consistent throughout your document you should only amend leading through the **Style sheet**.

Click on the style to be changed.

Click on **Change this style**.

Click on **Line spacing**.

Adjust the spacing to suit your document.

Paragraph space is adjusted here.

Amend text according to proof correction symbols

You will need to know the following proof correction symbols

Correction	Meaning	Symbol
stet	as it was	stet
insert	add	
new paragraph	begin a new paragraph	or
transpose	change around	
delete	remove	
close up	remove space	
capitalisation	change to upper case	
run on	make into one paragraph	

Insert text

Position your mouse and click in the position you wish to insert the text, then enter the text exactly as shown.

Creating a table

Click on 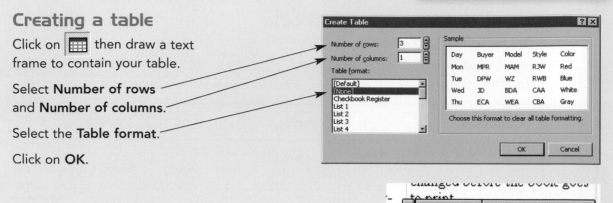 then draw a text frame to contain your table.

Select **Number of rows** and **Number of columns**.

Select the **Table format**.

Click on **OK**.

The table will be inserted.

Adjust the column widths by holding the mouse button on the column guide on the grey bar and sliding it to the chosen position.

Enter the text.

Click away from the table to return to normal view.

Copyfit publication

Check your document **very carefully**.

Subheadings must be kept with at least two lines of text.

There must be at least two lines of related text at the bottom and at the top of each column.

Spacing in styles must be consistently applied.

Generally, there must be no more than 10mm of white space anywhere in the document. For certain layouts you may be told that this rule does not apply to certain columns.

Lines, boxes, text and graphics must not touch or overlap unless you have been instructed to overlay them.

Automatic hyphenation can be turned off by clicking on **Tools**, then **Language** and selecting **Hyphenation**.

Saving a publication

Click on 🖫

Enter the name of your publication.

In the **Save as type** box, select **Publisher Files**.

Click **Save**.

Preparing a publication for press

Printing a publication

Click on **File**, **Print**, **Advanced Print Settings**.

Click on **Crop marks**, **Allow bleeds** and **Bleed marks**.

Click **OK**.

Printing colour-separated camera-ready copy

Click on **Tools**.

Select **Commercial Printing Tools** then **Colour Printing**.

Click in **Spot colour(s)**.

Click **OK**.

Click on **File, Print**.

Select **All pages**.

Click **Print separations**.

Click **OK**.

Printing composite proofs

Click on **File, Print**.

Select **All pages**.

Click **Print composite**.

Click **OK**.

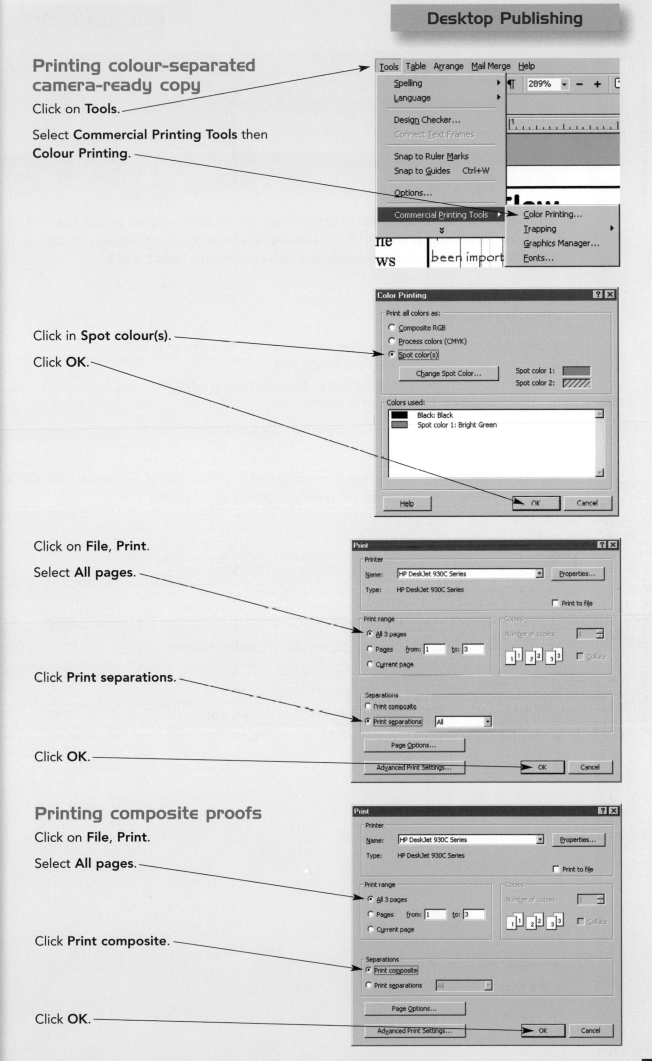

Build Up Exercises

TASK 1

This task is designed to allow you to practise some of the skills required to gain the OCR Level 2 Certificate for IT Users (CLAIT PLUS) assessment objectives for Unit 4 Desktop Publishing. To cover all the assessment objectives you will have to complete Tasks 2 and 3.

Before you begin

You should know how to:

- set up a master page and a style sheet according to a design brief
- import and manipulate text and image files
- amend your publication according to proof correction symbols
- print composite proofs.

Scenario

You are working for an entertainment company that organises parties and shows. You have been asked to provide an article about the history of clowns and clowning.

To produce the publication you will need the following files:

A text file: **birth**

Image files: **strip** and **bigfoot**

You will find these files on the CD that accompanies this book.

You will need to refer to the:

- House Style Sheet
- Page Layout Sheet

House Style Sheet – Tasks 1, 2 and 3

Page setup

- Use A4 paper
- Orientation: landscape
- Page size: 20.5 cm wide
                15 cm tall
- Margins: top   1 cm
                bottom   1 cm
                left   1 cm
                right   1 cm
- Gutter: 0.5 cm
- Header: flush to left   your name
- Footer: flush to right   your centre no

Text style

Feature	Font	Font size	Style	Alignment	Colour
Headline	serif	36	bold	centred	black
Subheadings	serif	12–16	italic	left	red
Body	serif	9–11		left	black
Bullet text	sans serif	9–11	italic	left	red
Table text	serif	7–9		left	red
Box text	sans serif	14–16		centred	black

Notes:

1   You **must** use **2 different** serif typefaces in the publication.

2   The subheadings in this assignment are:

Jesters
Commedia del Arte
Origins of the Auguste character
Joseph Grimaldi – The Father of Modern Clowning
Shakespeare's Clowns
The First Circus Clown
Singing Clowns

You have been asked to produce an article about the history of clowns and clowning. The text and graphics have already been produced. However, there are some errors in the text and you should make the amendments before or after you import it into your publication.

The exact positioning of the text and images is shown on the Page Layout sketches. Note the text flow, as not all the column space is to be used.

The publication will be produced in red and black. However, you do not need a colour printer, as you will be printing colour-separated pages.

What You Have To Do

Assessment Objectives		What You Have To Do
1a, 1b, 1c 1d, 1e, 1f	1	Create a new publication following the given page orientation and measurements exactly as shown on the attached Page Layout sketches.
1g	2	Set up the styles outlined on the House Style Sheet.
1h	3	Save the file as a master page.
3e, 3f	4	You should make the amendments shown on pages 81 and 82. You may do this work before you import the text file, or when you have brought it into your DTP package. Check your work carefully to ensure that you have made all the amendments shown. You will have to key in the text for the heading, as it is **not** included in the text file.
2a, 2b, 2c 2d, 2e, 2f 2g	5	Import the text file and images and place them as shown on the Page Layout sketches. The text should begin at the top of the left-hand column on the first page, below the heading.
2d, 2f, 3f	6	On the second page, in the middle column, create a shaded box and enter the text below into the box. Apply the box text style.

CALL TODAY
TO BOOK MELANIE AND ANGELO
FOR YOUR PARTY
0151 637 0161
OR VISIT
www.millasmagicalcircus.co.uk

Assessment Objectives		What You Have To Do
2d	7	In the paragraph below Commedia del Arte, apply bullet points to the text beginning: **The First Zany ...** **The Second Zany ...** **The Fantesca ...**
2d	8	Apply the house style to the publication as detailed in the House Style Sheet.
4a, 4d	9	Save and print a composite proof copy of the publication.

TASK 2

Before you begin

You should know how to:

- amend publication content
- create a table
- amend the leading.

You have been asked to make the following amendments, but note that you **must** use the **same fonts** and the **same point sizes** that you chose to use originally, unless otherwise instructed.

What You Have To Do

Assessment Objectives		
3a	1	Make the following changes:

Page	Item
First	Remove the dropped caps
Second	Crop the graphic **strip** so that the clown on the far left is removed. Resize the graphic to fill the original space
	Remove the dropped caps
	In the paragraph below the subheading **Commedia del Arte** delete the final sentence . . . **There were three types of comic servants:** and **all the bullet text**
Third	Remove the dropped caps
	Delete the subheading **Singing Clowns** and the paragraph below it beginning **In America**, . . .

3d, 3f   **2**   On the third page, at the bottom of the final column, create the following table. Apply the style specified on the House Style Sheet.

TYPE	COSTUME
Classic European	Generous – buttons or pompoms should be of a contrasting colour.
Straight Whiteface	Satins, sequins, rhinestones and theatrical fabrics (shiny, beaded,etc.). Shoes can be large or small but should be simple.
Auguste	A jacket or coat. Pants could be short, long, or oversize. Choose from a wide selection of colourful plaids, stripes, and polka dots, as well as solid colours. Lots of pockets and accessories.

1g   **3**   Change the following items on your style sheet:

Style name	Typeface	Point size	Alignment
Headline		42	
Body text			Justified

What You Have To Do

Assessment Objectives		
3b	4	Amend the leading of the body text so that the columns are balanced at the bottom of each page of the article. You should ensure that the text reaches to the bottom of *every* column.
		Ensure there is a visible difference in the leading from that used in the first print. You may resize the other objects to achieve this effect.
		Make sure that the middle column on the third page remains empty.
3c	5	Copyfit your publication to ensure:

- all material is displayed as specified
- text/graphics/lines are not superimposed on each other
- there are no widows and orphans
- paragraph spacing is consistent
- leading is consistent
- there are no hyphenated line endings
- white space appears only if specified in the Design Brief.

You may resize any/all images to assist in the copyfitting process.

4a, 4d	6	Save your work and print a composite proof to check your copyfitting.

TASK 3

Before you begin

You should know how to:

- prepare a publication for press.

What You Have To Do

Assessment Objectives		
4b, 4c	I	Prepare red and black colour separated prints showing crop marks.
		You must produce two printouts of each page, one for each colour. Be careful to ensure that each item of the publication appears on *either* the red printout *or* the black printout.
		Ensure that each page can be identified (ie Page 1 – Black, Page 1 – Red, Page 2 – Black, Page 2 – Red).
		Print the publication.

Text required for Tasks 1, 2 and 3

Since the dawn of history, clowns have held a privileged position within their hearts. They have been allowed relatively free commentary over political and individual issues, often reinforcing the very laws or rules they appear to ridicule. They were, and still are, openly encouraged to ignore or intentionally violate social and sacred customs and mores.

The art of clowning has existed for thousands of years. A clown performed as a jester in the court of the pharaohs in about 2500 BC. Court jesters have performed in China since 1818 BC. Throughout history most cultures have had clowns. In 1520 ad the Aztecs were found to include jesters similar to those in Europe.

Aristophanes, a political satirist of ancient Athens, wrote some of the earliest recorded comedies. He used his plays to portray the foolishness of governors and military leaders. He believed they were destroying the grandeur of Athens through their petty bickering, divisive leadership and endless wars with Sparta. His plays still call our attention to the ageless problems of politics, the battle of the sexes, the generation conflicts, crowded city life, pollution, traffic congestion, dishonesty and the wastefulness of government.

The Romans witnessed the telling of mythological stories based on dance and music and all without the use of the spoken word leading to the birth of pantomime. Curiously, the earliest pantomime performances more closely resembled a modern day combination of opera and ballet.

With the destruction of Rome in the late fifth century, the structured comedies all but vanished into the abyss of the dark ages and the performers became wandering beggars.

Jesters

Clowns who performed as court jesters were given great freedom of speech. Often they were the only one to speak out against the ruler's ideas, and through their humour were able to affect policy. In about 300 BC Chinese emperor Shih Huang-Ti oversaw the building of the Great Wall of China. Thousands of labourers were killed during its construction. He planned to have the wall painted which would have resulted in thousands more dying. His jester, Yu Sze, was the only one who dared criticize his plan. Yu Sze jokingly convinced him to abandon his plan. Yu Sze is remembered today as a Chinese national hero.

One of the most famous of the European court jesters was Nasir Ed Din. One day the king glimpsed himself in a mirror, and saddened at how old he looked, started crying. The other members of the court decided they better cry as well. When the king stopped crying, everyone else stopped crying as well, except Nasir Ed Din. When the king asked Nasir why he was still crying, he replied, "Sire, you looked at yourself in the mirror but for a moment and you cried. I have to look at you all the time."

Commedia del Arte

The Commedia del Arte began in Italy in the sixteenth century and soon dominated European theatre. It was a highly improvised theatre based upon stock characters and scenarios. It contained many comic characters divided into masters and servants. There were three types of comic servants:

The First Zany – a male servant who was a clever rogue, often plotting against his masters

The Second Zany – a stupid male servant who was caught up in the First Zany's schemes and often the victim of his pranks

The Fantesca – a female servant, played by an actress, who was a feminine version of one of the Zany characters and would participate in the schemes and provide a romantic story among the servants.

The history of clowning is one of creativity, evolution, and change. English pantomime is based on the Commedia del Arte.

Origins of the Auguste character

There is a widely told legend about the origins of the Auguste clown. According to the legend, an American acrobat named Tom Belling was performing with a circus in Germany in 1869. Confined to his dressing room as discipline for missing his tricks, he entertained his friends by putting on mis-fitting clothes to perform his impression of the show's manager. The manager suddenly entered the room. Belling ran away, ending up in the circus arena where he fell over the ring edge. In his embarrassment, and his haste to escape, he fell over the ring edge again on his way out. The audience yelled, "augustel" which is German for fool. The manager commanded that Belling continue appearing as the Auguste. Most serious historians doubt that the legend is true. For one thing, the word Auguste did not exist in the German language until after the character became popular. One of the theories of the true origin is that Belling copied the character from the R'izhii (red-haired) clowns he saw when he toured Russia.

Joseph Grimaldi – The Father of Modern Clowning

Joseph Grimaldi – (1778-1837) is considered to be the father of modern clowning because he is the entertainer who elevated the Whiteface clown to a starring role replacing Harlequin.

Grimaldi grew up in the theatre and excelled in the design of special effects. The type of production he starred in resembled live-action, with chase scenes.

Shakespeare's Clowns

During the reign of Queen Elizabeth, clowning in England was a theatrical art form. William Kemp was the first clown to appear with the troupe. William Kemp was such an important star that he was a part owner in both the troupe performing Shakespeare's works and the Globe Theatre. He specialized in playing stupid country-bumpkin type characters (a style that would later become known as the Auguste).

The First Circus Clown

In 1768, Philip Astley created (what is considered) the first circus in England. He also created the first circus clown act called Billy Buttons. The topical act was based on a popular tale of a tailor. It became a part of many circuses for 100 years. Variations of the routine with somebody coming out of the audience to attempt to ride a horse are still being performed in modern circuses.

Singing Clowns *during the mid-nineteenth century,*

In America before the invention of the radio, popular songs were spread across the country by singing clowns, who played an important role in the spreading and preserving musical culture. ~~They would sell the music and lyrics following a show.~~ *delete*

Images required for this publication

bigfoot

strip

Design Brief for Tasks 1, 2 and 3

Landscape Orientation

First page

← 20.5 cm →

BIRTH OF THE CLOWN ← Apply a box

15 cm

Start text file **birth** here

image **bigfoot**

Second page

◄ image **strip** here ► ← Apply a box

Fill this column with a **shaded box**. Use **reverse** text, and **rotate** it so that the top line is next to column 1

Third page

◄ image **strip** here ► ← Apply a box

Do **not** allow text to flow into this column

Use **dropped caps** after **each** of the subheadings

UNIT 5 Presentation Graphics

This unit is designed to test your ability to use presentation graphics software to format slides and timings to manipulate and present data. You will apply a specified house style and print your work in a variety of formats.

You may find it easier to undertake this unit if you have completed the Presentation Graphics unit at Level 1. If you have done so, you will already know how to:

- identify and use presentation graphics software correctly
- set up a slide layout
- select fonts and enter text
- format slides
- manage and print presentation files.

To pass this unit

You must complete the three-hour OCR-set assignment without making any critical errors, and with no more than three accuracy errors. If you do not achieve a Pass you may re-take the assessment using a different assignment.

You cannot claim more than one unit from the same application area towards the 3 optional units of the Level 2 qualification, due to an overlap in content – ie you may choose one from Unit 5 Presentation Graphics, Unit 13 Presentation Graphics Solutions or Unit 20 Presentation Graphics (Microsoft Office Specialist Powerpoint Core/Comprehensive).

Your work will be marked by your tutor, and externally moderated by OCR.

Critical errors

- A missing slide.
- Data being incorrectly imported or inserted.
- Failure to insert any specified graphic(s).
- Failure to embed the specified chart.
- Failure to embed the specified organisation chart.
- Failure to hide slide(s).
- Failure to create hyperlink to access hidden slide(s).

Accuracy errors

- Each instance of an error in entering data. In this unit apply one data entry error for any error(s) in a title, a line of text, a label in a chart or a label in an organisation chart. Numeric data for the chart must be entered with a 100% accuracy.
- Each instance of an error in completing an assessment objective.

What will you learn?

When you have completed this unit you should be able to:

- create a presentation
- set up a master slide
- insert and manipulate data
- control a presentation
- support a presentation.

How to meet the assessment objectives

You will be introduced to **one** method of achieving the assessment objectives. There will be other methods of carrying out these tasks. Only objectives that were not covered in Level 1 are included.

You will already know how to set up a slide layout, select fonts and enter text, format slides, manage and print presentation files.

Now we will deal with the new areas.

The basics

Adding a slide

To create a chart on a slide, go to **Common Tasks** on the toolbar.

Click the down arrow.

Click **New Slide**.

Deleting a slide

Go to the slide you want to delete.

Click **Edit**, **Delete Slide**.

Hiding a slide

Select the slide to be hidden.

Click **Slide Show, Hide Slide**.

Repeat the process to display the slide again.

Setting up a master slide layout and style in accordance with specified house style

Applying background colour

Click **Format, Background**.

In **Background Fill** click the down arrow.

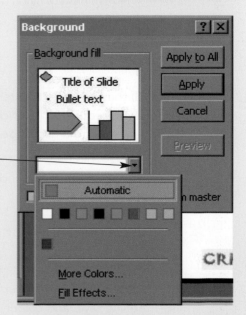

To change the colour click on any colour under **Automatic**

or

Click **More Colours**.

Select from the palette. ——————

Click **OK**.

Click **Apply**.

To change the colour for all the slides, click **Apply to All**.

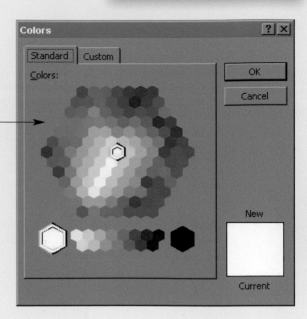

Importing, inserting and manipulating data, graphics and slides

Embedding an organisation chart

To create an organisation chart on a new slide, go to **Common Tasks**.

Click the down arrow.

Click **New Slide**.

Select **Organisation chart**. —

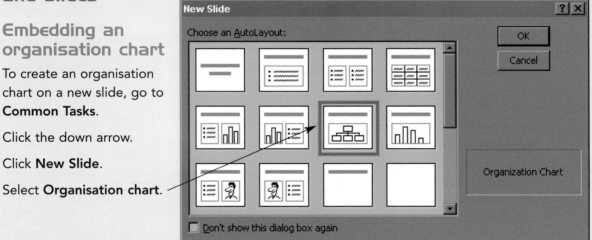

Double click on the graphic to add the ——— organisation chart.

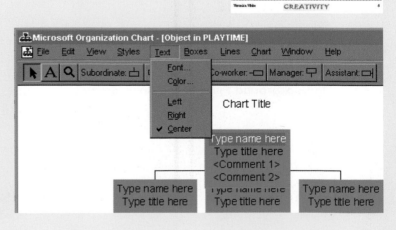

You will then be able to enter the details you require for your chart including making any changes to:

- the style of chart
- the number of levels and boxes
- the text
  - font
  - colour
  - alignment
- the box style and colour
- the line style and colour

Embedding a chart

To create a chart on a slide, go to **Common Tasks**.

Click the down arrow.

Click **New Slide**.

Select Chart.

Click **OK**.

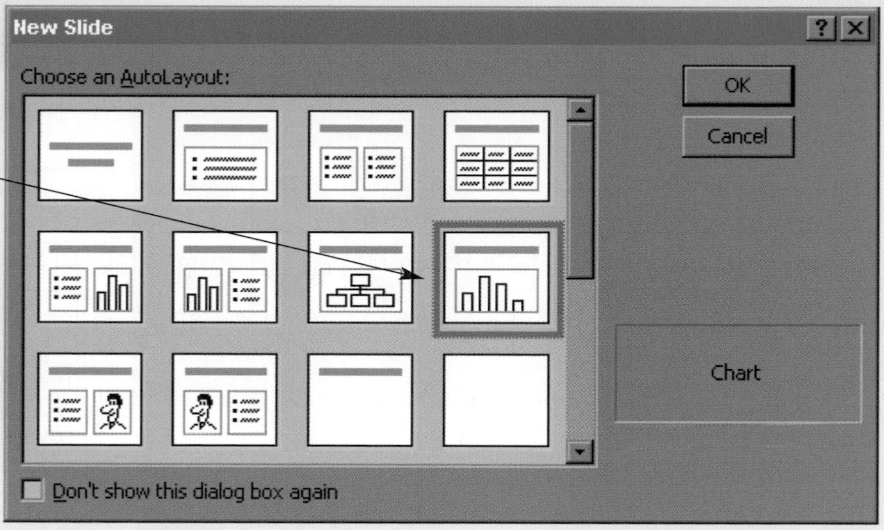

The program will provide a column chart as the default.

Double click to add a chart.

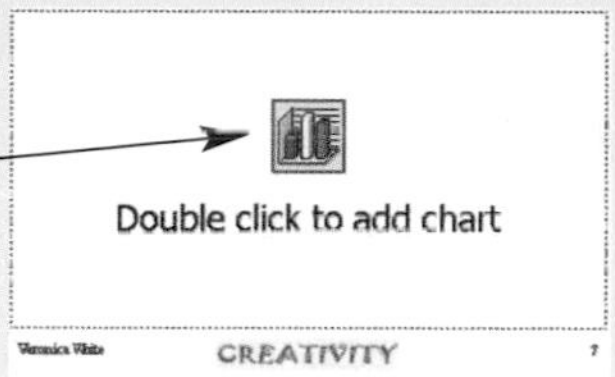

Double click to add chart

CREATIVITY

You will now also see the data used to create the chart.

You can either key in your own data in this box

or

Import the data.

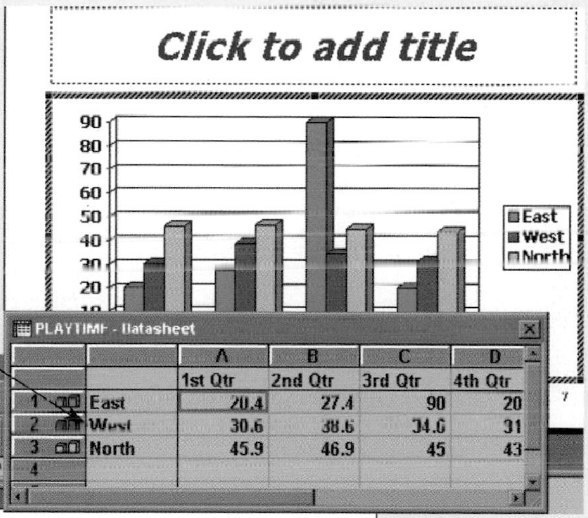

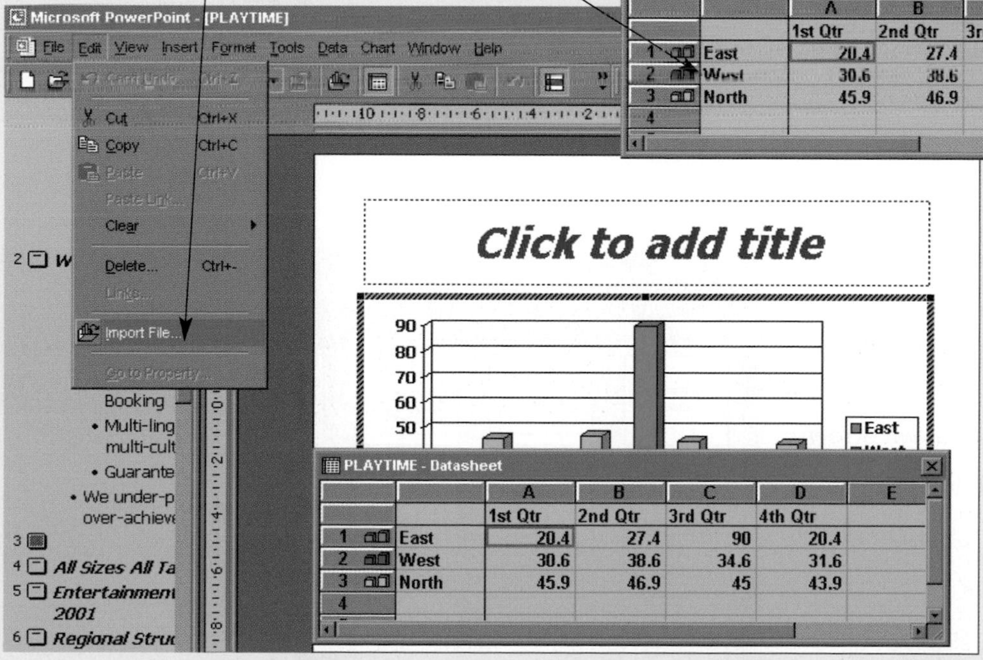

If you want to change the chart **type** (eg to a pie chart):

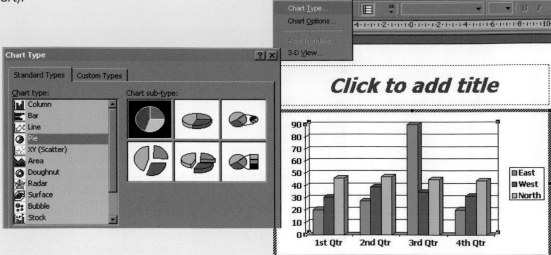

Click on the chart.

Click **Chart**, **Chart Type**.

Click **Standard Types**, **Pie**.

Click **OK**.

To add or change any details on the chart – eg title, legend or labels – click on the chart.

Click **Chart**, **Chart Options**.

Enter the details you require.

Click OK.

The chart will be displayed with a border on the plot area.

To remove the border, double-click on the Plot area.

The **Format Plot Area** screen will appear.

In the **Border** box, click the **None** box.

Click **OK**.

Using tables

To create a table on a slide, go to **Common Tasks**.

Click the down arrow.

Click **New Slide**.

Select Table.

Click **OK**.

On the slide, double click to add the table.

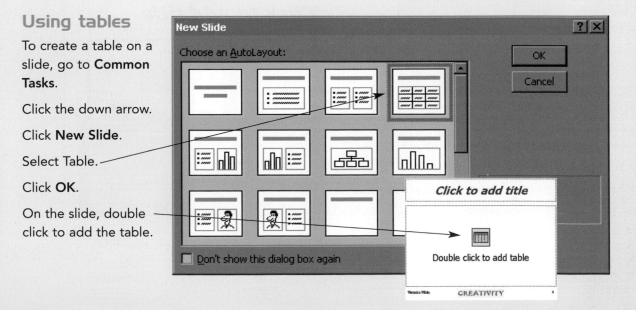

You will be required to specify

Number of columns

Number of rows.

Click **OK**.

Insert Table

Number of columns:
2
Number of rows:
2

OK
Cancel

Enter the text as required.

You can adjust the size of the boxes by clicking and dragging on the lines.

Click to add title

Inserting slide numbers, the date and your name

Click **View, Master, Slide Master**.

View Insert Format Tools Slide Show Window H

Normal
Slide Sorter
Notes Page
Slide Show   F5

Master
Header and Footer...

Slide Master
Title Master
Handout Master
Notes Master

Times New R

Click **View, Header and Footer**.

Click for **Date and time**.

Header and Footer

Slide | Notes and Handouts

Include on slide
☑ Date and time
○ Update automatically
7/8/02
Language: Calendar type:
English (U.S.)   Western

Apply to All
Apply
Cancel

Enter your name.

Click **Slide number**.

Check the **Preview**.

Click **Apply to All**.

○ Fixed
Veronica White
☑ Slide number
☑ Footer

Preview

☐ Don't show on title slide

Controlling a presentation

Applying transitions and effects

Go to the Slide Sorter view.

Move to the first slide.

On the toolbar click in the first box to display the **transitions** available and make your selection.

Move to the next box to display the **effects** available and make your selection.

Move to the next slide and repeat the steps above.

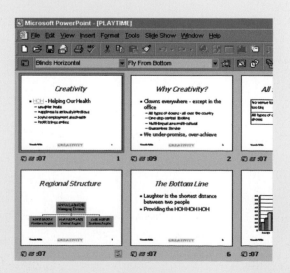

Applying timings

From either **Normal** or **Slide Sorter** view:

Select the slide or slides you want to set the timing for.

Click **Slide Show**, **Slide Transition**.

Under **Advance**, click **Automatically after**.

Enter the number of seconds the slide should appear on the screen.

To apply the timing to the selected slides, click **Apply**.

To apply the timing to all the slides, click **Apply to All**.

Changing the order of slides

You can easily change the order of slides in the Slide Sorter view.

Click the slide.

Drag and place in new position.

Creating a hyperlink to access a hidden slide

On the source slide, highlight the text to be used for the hyperlink.

Go to **Insert Hyperlink** icon.

Select **Place in This Document**.

Specify the destination in the document.

Click **OK**.

Printing presentation documents

Click **File, Print**.

You can print **All**, **Current** or **Selection**.

You can select any of the following options for printing:

- Slides
- Handouts (any number per page)
- Notes Pages
- Outline View

You can also select other options such as Print hidden slides.

Providing a screen print to show use of special effects and timings

You will have to make a screen print to provide the evidence that you have applied the special effects, and timings.

Click **View, Slide Sorter**.

Press the key marked **PrtScr** or **PrintScrn** on your keyboard.

Open Word, and a blank document should appear on your screen.

Click on the right mouse button, click **Paste**.

A copy should appear on your screen. Add your name and the date.

Save your file and print a copy. Close your file and Word.

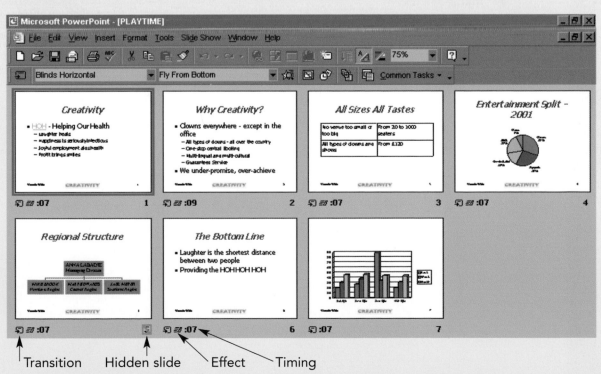

Transition   Hidden slide   Effect   Timing

Build Up Exercises

This task is designed to allow you to practise some of the skills required to gain the OCR Level 2 Certificate for IT Users (CLAIT PLUS) assessment objectives for Unit 5 Presentation Graphics. To cover all the assessment objectives you will have to complete Tasks 2 and 3.

Before you begin

You should know how to:

- create a presentation
- set up a master slide
- insert and manipulate data
- print all slides on one page.

Scenario

You are working for an entertainment company that organises parties and shows. It provides different types of clowns and circus-style acts.

The Marketing Manager is always looking for new markets. One market niche is the medical sector. He has arranged to make a presentation at a medical conference. He has provided you with all the text and images.

The text and images are in the following files:

- Slide text file: **clopres**
- Speaker's notes text file: **clospeak**
- Image file: **cloim**

You will find these files on the CD that accompanies this book.

You will apply the styles on the House Style Sheet to your presentation.

House Style Sheet

Master slide

Feature	Colour	Style	Position	Additional information
Background	white			
Graphic			bottom, centre	in the footer
Slide no	black	any	bottom, right	in the footer
Text	black	any	bottom, left	in the footer designer's name
Timings				Slide 2 9 seconds remaining slides 7 seconds
Slide transitions				1 transition effect on every slide
Custom animations (Build effects)				1 build effect on every slide except the table and final blank slide

Text

Style name	Typeface	Point size	Feature	Colour	Alignment
Heading/Title	sans serif	46	bold and italic	red	centre
First level (bullet text)	sans serif	36	to include a bullet character	black	left
Second level (sub-bullet text)	sans serif	26	to include a bullet character	black	left

Table

Style name	Typeface	Point size	Feature	Colour	Alignment
Text	sans serif	28	no bullet characters	black	left
Currency	sans serif	28	0 decimal places	black	

Pie chart

Style name	Typeface	Point size	Feature	Colour	Alignment
Data labels	sans serif	14	bold and italic	black	

Organisation chart

Style name	Typeface	Point size	Feature	Colour	Alignment
Top level text box	serif	22		black	centre
2nd level text box	serif	20	italic	black	centre
Boxes			show borders	black	
Lines				red	

Speaker's notes

Style name	Typeface	Point size	Feature	Colour	Alignment
Text	sans serif	16		black	left

What You Have To Do

Assessment Objectives		
1a, 2a, 2b, 2c, 2d, 2e	1	Open your presentation graphics software. Set up a Master Slide using the sketch below and the House Style Sheet:

SET AND APPLY HEADING STYLE

SET AND APPLY

BULLET AND

SUB-BULLET STYLES

YOUR NAME   IMAGE cloim   SLIDE NUMBER

1b, 3a	2	Open the text file **clopres**. Insert the text for all the slides as indicated, eg

Slide 1

HEADING
Creativity

Bullets
HOH – Helping Our Health

Sub-bullets
Laughter heals
Happiness is seriously infectious
Joyful employment aids health

Save the presentation with the name **Medical**.

5c	3	Print an overview of the 5 slides on one page.

TASK 2

Before you begin

You should know how to:

- control and support a presentation.

You have been asked to make several modifications that will allow the presentation to be used at more than one function.

What You Have To Do

Assessment Objectives		
2a, 2b, 2c, 2d, 2e, 3a, 3b, 3f	1	Modify Slide 3 – **All Sizes All Tastes**. Use an appropriate slide layout to produce a 2-column table showing the data below.

No venue too small or too big	From 20 to 1000 seaters
All types of magicians and shows	From £120

Apply the house style.

Assessment Objectives		
2a, 2b, 2c, 2d, 2e, 3d, 3h	2	Insert a new slide as Slide 5. Use an appropriate slide layout to enable the creation of a chart on the slide.

Make the slide heading **Entertainment Split – 2001**

Use the chart template to create a pie chart with the following data:

Clowns	72
Puppets	63
Comic Ballet	36
Stilts	48
Circus	17

The chart must *not* display a legend but *must* display data labels and % values.

Apply the house style.

3h	3	Delete the current Slide 4 – **Innovative and Original**.
2b, 3a, 3b	4	Make the following amendments:

Slide	Title	Action
1	Creativity	Add, as the last line, the sub-bullet text: **Profit brings smiles**
2	Why Creativity?	Add as bullet text **after** sub-bullets: **We under-promise, over-achieve**
5	The Bottom Line	Add, as the **first** bullet, the text: **Laughter is the shortest distance between two people**

What You Have To Do

Assessment Objectives

2a, 2b, 2c, 2d, 2e, 3e, 3h	5	Insert a new Slide 6. Use an appropriate slide layout to enable the creation of an organisation chart. Insert the slide heading **Regional Structure**, and enter the data.

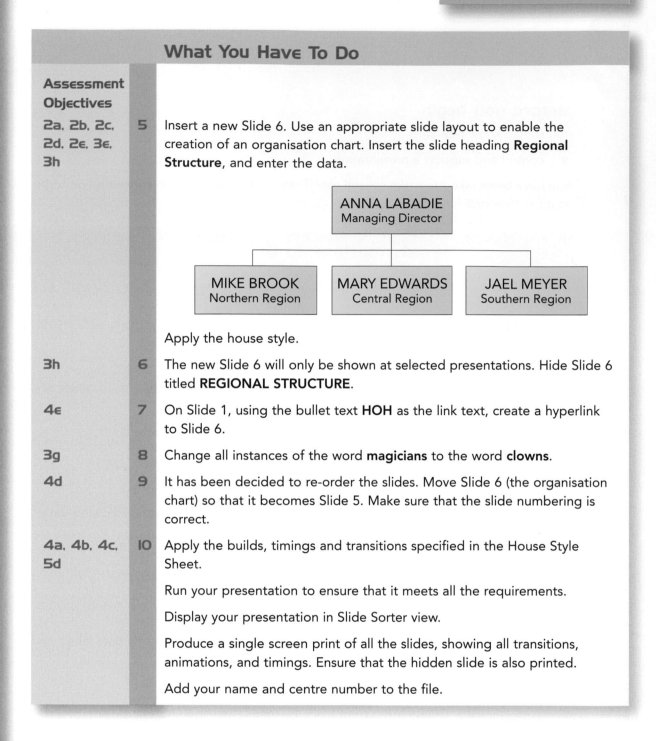

Apply the house style.

3h	6	The new Slide 6 will only be shown at selected presentations. Hide Slide 6 titled **REGIONAL STRUCTURE**.
4e	7	On Slide 1, using the bullet text **HOH** as the link text, create a hyperlink to Slide 6.
3g	8	Change all instances of the word **magicians** to the word **clowns**.
4d	9	It has been decided to re-order the slides. Move Slide 6 (the organisation chart) so that it becomes Slide 5. Make sure that the slide numbering is correct.
4a, 4b, 4c, 5d	10	Apply the builds, timings and transitions specified in the House Style Sheet.

Run your presentation to ensure that it meets all the requirements.

Display your presentation in Slide Sorter view.

Produce a single screen print of all the slides, showing all transitions, animations, and timings. Ensure that the hidden slide is also printed.

Add your name and centre number to the file.

TASK 3

Before you begin

You should know how to:

- support a presentation.

You will have to access the text file **clospeak**. You will find the file on the CD that accompanies this book.

What You Have To Do

Assessment Objectives		
2a, 2b, 3a	1	You have been asked to produce Speaker's notes. Open the text file **clospeak**. It contains the text for the Speaker's notes. Insert the text as indicated, eg Slide 1 HEADING Creativity Creativity is in the business of making life fun. The truisms Laughter heals Happiness is seriously infectious Joyful employment aids health are not just an old wives tale. A positive mental attitude mixed with laughter keeps us all healthy Apply the house style.
5a, 5b	2	Provide the following printouts of Slides **1** and **6 only**: Individual slides Speaker's notes
3a, 3h	3	It has been decided to add a Title slide as the first slide and a final blank slide to complete the presentation. Do **not** show your name or the slide number **in the footer** on the new slides. Make the **Title slide** with the following text: **Creativity Briefing Day** **Your name**
1b, 5d, 5e	4	Save your presentation. Provide the following printouts: An **outline** print showing the text on all the slides A single screen print from the **Slide Sorter** view of all the slides. Ensure that the hidden slide is printed. Add your name and centre number to the file.

UNIT 6 Computer Art

This unit is designed to test your ability to use graphic editing and design software to create artwork for a variety of purposes, including printed and electronic media. You will become familiar with editing concepts, common software tools, and the requirements of the destination media. You will have to use a colour printer for the output from this unit.

You may find it easier to undertake this unit if you have completed the Computer Art unit at Level 1. If you have done so, you will already know how to:

- identify and use appropriate software correctly
- import, crop and resize images
- enter, amend and resize text
- manipulate and format page items
- manage and print artwork.

To pass this unit

You must complete the three-hour OCR-set assignment without making any critical errors, and with no more than three accuracy errors. If you do not achieve a Pass you may re-take the assessment using a different assignment.

Your work will be marked by your tutor, and externally moderated by OCR.

Critical errors

- A missing or incorrect image.
- A missing text item (in entirety).
- A missing frame in an animation.
- Failure to print in colour.
- A missing frame duration.

Accuracy errors

- Each instance of an error in entering data. In this unit apply one data entry error for any error(s) in each word.
- Each instance of an error in completing an assessment objective.

What will you learn?

When you have completed this unit you should be able to:

- create artwork incorporating text and images in layers
- edit and retouch scanned images
- use a variety of graphic effects
- create an animated image for electronic media
- prepare artwork for print/electronic publishing.

For this unit we will be using Microsoft Photodraw V2 and GIF Animator.

Background information

Microsoft Office 2000 Premium includes PhotoDraw V2 and FrontPage. The standalone versions of FrontPage 98 and FrontPage 2000 includes Image Composer 1.5 with GIF Animator (designed to work with it to produce animations). FrontPage 2002 includes neither but does include 'PowerPoint Like Drawing Tools'.

Microsoft Photodraw V2 has been withdrawn.

GIF Animator, now Microsoft freeware, can only be downloaded from non-Microsoft Internet sites. One such place is http://www.rocketdownload.com/Details/Inte/4282.htm

If you do not have any of the above pieces of software, you may not know which program to use. These are some of the possibilities:

Software		Price
Microsoft Picture It!	For those who want something that is about as simple as it gets. It is less expensive, but still has the necessary set of features. You will also still need to use GIF Animator.	£25–35
Adobe PhotoShop Elements	Adobe has taken 'elements' (some of the best features) from Photoshop and made them easier to use for those who do not use graphics for a living. It has all the necessary features without facing the complexities of Photoshop itself. 80% of PhotoShop's power at 20% of the price.	£35–70
JASC Paint Shop Pro 7.0 (includes Animation Shop)	Almost PhotoShop power, but much cheaper. Steeper learning curve than either PhotoShop Elements or Picture It! but does more. Shareware versions can be downloaded from www.jasc.com or www.tucows.com and online registration costs $99. A boxed retail version costs around £90.	£0–£90

Microsoft Photodraw V2

You will be required to set the resolution (picture quality) before printing. In the assignment this is expressed as dpi.

In Microsoft Photodraw V2 it is not expressed in this way, but the equivalents are:

Web	96 dpi
Typical (Photographic)	150 dpi
Professional (Best for printing)	300 dpi

How to meet the assessment objectives

You will be introduced to **one** method of achieving the assessment objectives. There will be other methods of carrying out these tasks. Only objectives that were not covered in Level 1 are included.

You will already know how to import, crop and resize images, enter, amend and resize text, manipulate and format page items, manage and print artwork.

Now we will deal with the new areas.

Creating artwork incorporating text and images in layers

Layering items

As you add **objects** to your work they are ordered from front to back – the foremost object covers a portion of objects behind it.

You can add as many objects as you like, and change the order by clicking **Arrange**, **Order**.

Save in the program file type (.**mix**) to continue to edit your work. If you use the **gif** or **jpg** format this is not possible.

Click **Insert** to bring in previously stored text or images.

Click **Text** to enter your own text.

Editing and retouching scanned images

Removing dust

Select the object on which you want to work.

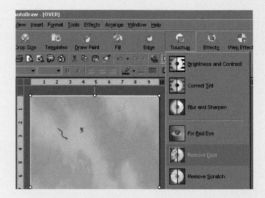

Zoom in to magnify the dust.

Click **Touchup**, **Remove Dust**.

Click on the dust to remove.

On the **Dust and Spots** toolbar click **Finish**.

Removing scratches

Select the object on which you want to work.

Zoom in to magnify the scratches.

Click **Touchup**, **Remove Scratch**.

Under **Scratch width**, click a width on the slider.

On the first scratch click the **starting point**, then click the **end point**.

On the **Scratch toolbar** click **Finish**.

Removing unwanted content

We will go through two methods of removing content:

1   Using colour matching

Select the object on which you want to work.

Zoom in to magnify the area (**200%**).

Click **Crop Size**, **Cut Out**, **By Colour**.

Click on the areas you want to cut out. As you click on each area it will change colour.

When you have selected all the areas, on the **Cut Out** toolbar, click **Finish**.

2 Using the edge finder

Select the object on which you want to work.

Zoom in to magnify the area (**200%**).

Click **Crop Size**, **Cut Out**, **Edge Finder**.

Go to any point on the shape you want to cut out and click. The yellow diamond will mark this start position.

Move around the edge and click. As you do you will see the edge outlined by a broken black line.

When you get back to the start position, on the **Cut Out** toolbar, click **Finish**.

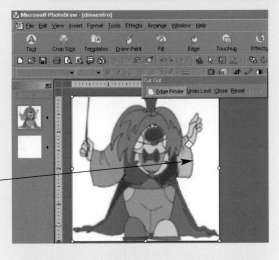

Using a variety of graphic effects

Setting image transparency

Select the object on which you want to work.

Click **Effects**, **Transparency**.

You can adjust the transparency by:

using the slide bar
using the arrows in the box showing %

Close the transparency box.

Setting hue, saturation and brightness

Select the object on which you want to work.

Click **Effects**, **Colour Effects**, **Colourize**, **Hue and Saturation**.

Adjust:

Hue
Saturation
Brightness

Close the **Colour** box.

Using solid, gradient or pattern fills

Select the object on which you want to work – in this case a box.

Click **Format, Fill, Two-Colour Gradient**.

Select:

Start colour

End colour

Shape

Close the **Fill** box.

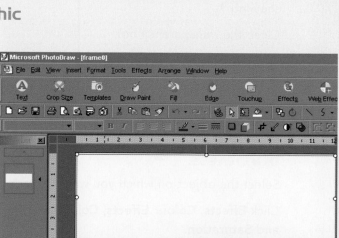

Applying a drop shadow

Select the object on which you want to work – in this case a box.

Click **Effects, Shadow**.

Select the shadow type.

Close the **Shadow** box.

Creating an animated image for electronic media

Creating individual frames using text, images and graphic shapes

Creating a basic frame layout

To create an animation you first have to create each of the **frames**.

Create the basic frame layout, including the **size** of the frame and the **background**.

Save this file as **frame0** in **gif format**.

You can then use this basic frame as the source for any other frame in the sequence.

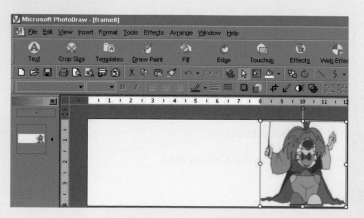

Creating other frames in the sequence.

Open frame0 and insert the text and images for use in that frame, in the specified positions.

Save the new frame with the new frame number (eg frame1, frame2, etc).

Repeat this process until all the frames are complete.

Creating a new animation

When you have all the frames ready, you **will have to use the program GIF Animator to compose your animation**.

Note: Because of the way this program works, it is easier to put your animation together in **reverse** order. For example, from frame 7 back to frame 1 (if there are 7 frames).

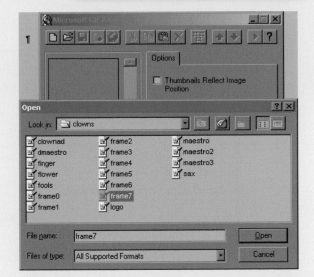

Open frame7

Insert	frame6
	frame5
	frame4
	frame3
	frame2
	frame1

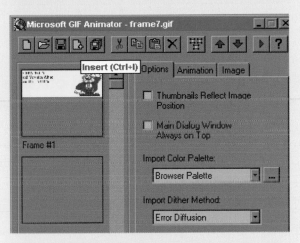

When all the frames in the sequence have been inserted

Save As (filename) in **gif** format.

Setting the duration of frames

Go to the **Image** tab.

Enter details for:

Duration

Transition choice

Transparency

You will have to make
these choices on **every** frame.

Save your file.

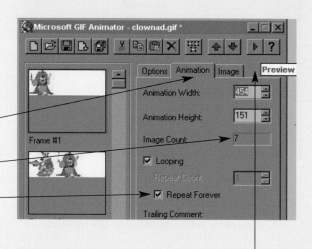

Saving the animation size

You set the animation size when you create
the basic frame, and it will be saved when
you save that frame. You then use the basic
frame, and therefore the size, for all the other
frames.

Go to the **Animation** tab where you can
check the size.

The number of frames is shown.

You can also set the number of times the
animation will run. Click on **Looping** and
Repeat Forever for continuous running.

To check your animation, go to the **Preview**
button.

Your animated gif will then run for you to see
the results.

Preparing artwork for print or electronic publishing

Setting resolution

Click **Tools, Options, Picture Quality**.

Click **Typical (Photographic)**.

Click **OK**.

Saving the artwork animation in appropriate format

Insert all the frames for your animation into your file.

Enter the filename.

You must save it in **gif** format.

Printing a full colour proof, displaying crop marks

Click **File, Print**.

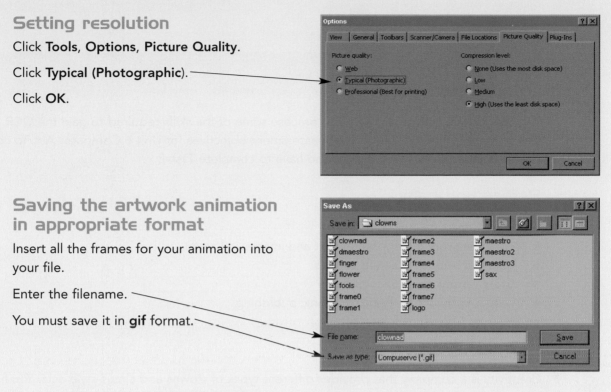

Click **Print crop marks**.

Click **OK**.

Build Up Exercises

TASK 1

This task is designed to allow you to practise some of the skills required to gain the OCR Level 2 Certificate for IT Users (CLAIT PLUS) assessment objectives for Unit 6 Computer Art. To cover all the assessment objectives you will also have to complete Task 2.

Before you begin

You should know how to:

- create artwork incorporating text and images in layers
- edit and retouch scanned images
- use a variety of graphic effects
- prepare artwork for print/electronic publishing.

Scenario

Creativity is a company that provides different types of clowns and circus-style acts. You have been asked to produce some draft advertising material for the company. Your first task is to create the artwork for a direct mail poster. Your second task is to create a computer animation for an e-mail advertising campaign.

Before you start your tasks make sure that you have access to the following image files:

clouds, dmaestro, maestro2, maestro3, logo.

You will find these files on the CD that accompanies this book.

What You Have To Do

Assessment Objectives		
Ia	I	Create a new piece of artwork using the dimensions given in the Design Brief.
Ib, Ic, 5b	2	Import the image file **clouds**. Set the size of the image to cover the whole area of the artwork as a background. Save your file using the name **creative**.
2a	3	Remove noticeable dust and scratches from the top half of the picture.
2c	4	Adjust the hue and saturation of the image so that it has white clouds on a blue sky. You will have to adjust the Brightness to achieve this.
2b, 3a, 5b	5	Open the image file **dmaestro**. Apply an image mask to the image to remove the background. Save this new image as **maestro.gif**. You *must* use the **gif** format as you will be using this file again in another task that requires the **gif** format.

What You Have To Do

Assessment Objectives		
1b, 1c	6	Copy the **maestro** image into your **creative** file as a new layer and move it to position **maestro** as shown on the Design Brief. The image should be 4 cm by 4 cm.
1b, 1c, 3b	7	Import the image **maestro2** into your **creative** file. Make the following changes: • adjust the size to be 3 cm by 3 cm • position it as shown on the Design Brief • adjust the transparency to 30%.
1b, 1c, 3b	8	Import the image **maestro3** into your **creative** file. Make the following changes: • adjust the size to be 2 cm by 2 cm • position it as shown on the Design Brief • adjust the transparency to 50%.
3c, 3d	9	The **colour gradient box** shown on the Design Brief is a rectangular box 10 cm wide and 4 cm high. • create this box and locate it as shown on the Design Brief • format the box as follows: • no outside line • fill the box with a two-colour gradient running from white at the top to orange at the bottom • soften the edges of the box • apply a drop shadow that drops down to the right.
1b	10	Import the image **logo** and locate it as shown on the Design Brief.
1d, 3e	11	Create a **text box** for the slogan as shown on the Design Brief, and enter this text (in black) in it: **for all your clowning needs call (your name) on 0151 199 1066**
5a, 5e	12	Set the resolution (or picture quality) of your artwork to be 144 dpi or Typical (Photographic) quality (150 dpi). Produce a screen print of the dialogue box displaying the resolution settings. Add your name to this printout.
5b	13	Save your artwork.
5c, 5d	14	Print a colour proof copy showing crop marks.
	15	Close your files – **creative** and **maestro**.

TASK 2

Before you begin

You should know how to:

- create an animated image for electronic media.

 Before you start your task make sure that you have access to the following image files: **flower, sax, finger.** You will find these files on the CD accompanying this book.

You will also need access to the file **maestro**, which you created in Task 1.

Your second task is to create a computer animation for an e-mail advertising campaign.

What You Have To Do

Assessment Objectives		
4d	1	Set the new picture size as shown on the Design Brief.
3c, 4b	2	Insert a rectangle to fill the picture. The rectangle edge and fill should be yellow.
5b	3	Save your work as a **gif** file using the name **frame0**. Close the file.
5b	4	Open **frame0** and save as a **gif** file using the name **frame1**.
4b, 5b	5	Insert the image file **maestro** and place it as shown in the Design Brief. Save and close **frame1**.
5b	6	Open **frame0** and save as a **gif** file using the name **frame2**.
4b, 5b	7	Insert the image files **maestro** and **flower** and place them as shown in the Design Brief. Save and close **frame2**.
5b	8	Open **frame0** and save as a **gif** file using the name **frame3**.
4b, 5b	9	Insert the image files **maestro**, **flower** and **sax** and place them as shown in the Design Brief. Save and close **frame3**.
5b	10	Open **frame0** and save as a **gif** file using the name **frame4**.
4b, 5b	11	Insert the image files **flower**, **sax** and **finger** and place them as shown in the Design Brief. Save and close **frame4**.

What You Have To Do

Assessment Objectives		
5b	12	Open **frame0** and save as a **gif** file using the name **frame5**.
4b, 5b	13	Insert the image files **sax** and **finger**. Add the text **CREATIVITY** and place the text and images as shown in the Design Brief. Save and close **frame5**.
5b	14	Open **frame0** and save as a **gif** file using the name **frame6**.
4b, 5b	15	Insert the image file **finger**. Add the text **CREATIVITY** and **for all your clowning needs**. Place the text and images as shown in the Design Brief. Save and close **frame6**.
5b	16	Open **frame0** and save as a **gif** file using the name **frame7**.
4b, 5b	17	Insert the image file **finger**. Add the text **CREATIVITY** and **call (your name) on 0151 199 1066**. Place the text and images as shown in the Design Brief. Save and close **frame7**.
		You will now need to use the program **GIF Animator** to compose your animation.
		Note: Because of the way this program works, it is easier to put your animation together in **reverse** order – ie **open** frame7 and then **insert** frames 6 to 1.
4a	18	Load the program and **open frame7**. **Insert** frames 6 to 1.
4c	19	Set the frame duration and transitions as shown on the Design Brief.
5b	20	Save the animation in **gif** format, to enable publishing on the web. Save your work as **clownad**.
5e	21	You should check the animation before publishing it. Produce a screen print (or prints) displaying the 7 frames and:

- the timings
- the filenames
- the file extensions.

Design Brief for Computer Artwork

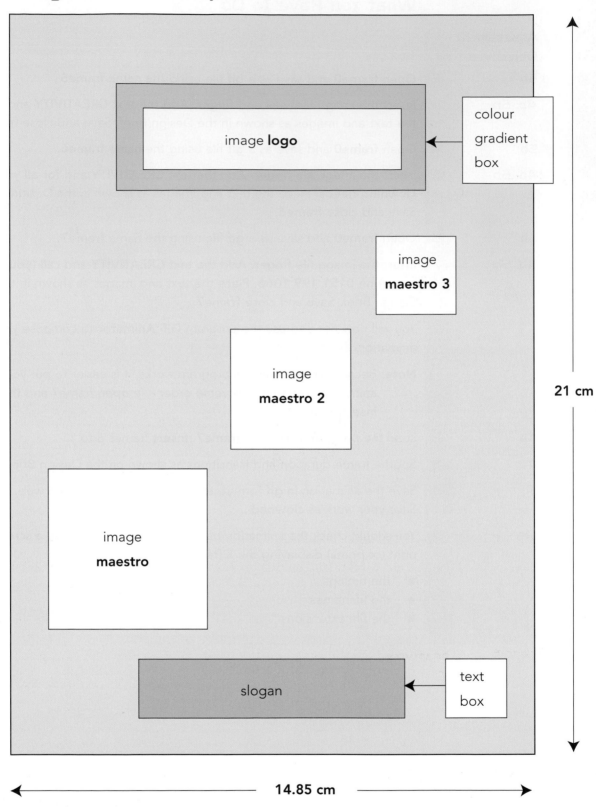

Design Brief for Computer Animation

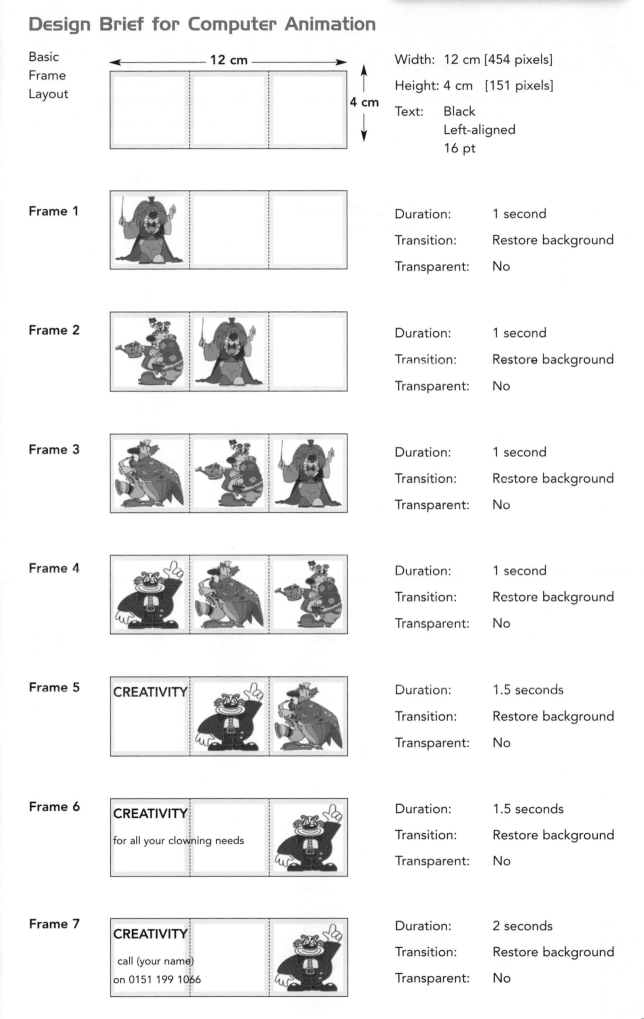

Basic Frame Layout

← 12 cm →

4 cm

Width: 12 cm [454 pixels]

Height: 4 cm [151 pixels]

Text: Black
Left-aligned
16 pt

Frame 1

Duration: 1 second

Transition: Restore background

Transparent: No

Frame 2

Duration: 1 second

Transition: Restore background

Transparent: No

Frame 3

Duration: 1 second

Transition: Restore background

Transparent: No

Frame 4

Duration: 1 second

Transition: Restore background

Transparent: No

Frame 5

CREATIVITY

Duration: 1.5 seconds

Transition: Restore background

Transparent: No

Frame 6

CREATIVITY

for all your clowning needs

Duration: 1.5 seconds

Transition: Restore background

Transparent: No

Frame 7

CREATIVITY

call (your name)

on 0151 199 1066

Duration: 2 seconds

Transition: Restore background

Transparent: No

UNIT 7 Web Page Creation

This unit is designed to test your ability to use software to select, present, manipulate and amend data for the Internet. You will use common HTML concepts and features, web page formatting and web site structure.

You may find it easier to undertake this unit if you have completed the Web Page Creation unit at Level 1. If you have done so, you will already know how to:

- identify and use appropriate software correctly
- import and place text and image files
- amend and format web pages
- insert relative, external and e-mail hyperlinks
- manage and print web pages.

To pass this unit

You must complete the three-hour OCR-set assignment without making any critical errors, and with no more than three accuracy errors. If you do not achieve a Pass you may re-take the assessment using a different assignment.

The practice assignments you carry out use files on the CD. When you carry out the assignment for assessment you will be given instructions to download files from OCR.

Your work will be marked by your tutor, and externally moderated by OCR.

Critical errors

- A link is missing.
- A link is not working.
- Specified text file missing in its entirety.
- A missing image.
- A form is not working (incorrectly specified method, incorrectly specified action, incorrectly specified hidden field, missing submit button, a submit button not correctly linked to opening form tag).

Accuracy errors

- Each instance of an error in entering data. In this unit apply one data entry error for any error(s) in a title, a meta tag, a line of text that will be used as a link, 'alt' text, a drop down list, or a word.
- Each instance of an error in completing an assessment objective.

What will you learn?

When you have completed this unit you should be able to:

- create web pages from unformatted source material
- use standard images and formatting to create a consistent house style
- create and format tables and forms
- use meta tags to define content
- set dimensions, alignment and other attributes of page items.

How to meet the assessment objectives

You will be introduced to **one** method of achieving the assessment objectives. There will be other methods of carrying out these tasks. Only objectives that were not covered in Level 1 are included.

You will already know how to import and place text and image files, amend and format web pages, insert relative, external and e-mail hyperlinks, manage and print web pages.

Now we will deal with the new areas.

Creating, formatting and saving web pages

Download files

You will need to download files to use on your web site. Load your Internet browser and locate the web site that contains the files you wish to download. Position the mouse over the file you wish to download and click on the right mouse button.

For a picture select **Save Picture As**.

For a text file select **Save Target As**.

You will see a **File Download** window, followed by the **Save As** window.

Locate the folder in which you want to save the file. Click on **Save**.

Note: These files must be stored in your web page folder. You should save your image files in the images subfolder.

Creating and defining web pages

Create a folder for your web pages with a subfolder for the images. Make sure you save all your work **within** your web pages folder.

Load **FrontPage**, a new web page will be opened.

Use meta tags to describe page content

Position your mouse on your web page, click on the right mouse button, and select **Page Properties**.

Click on **Custom**, then on **Add**.

Enter the meta tag **Name**, eg author, title or description.

Enter the content in **Value**, eg your name and centre number.

Click on **OK**.

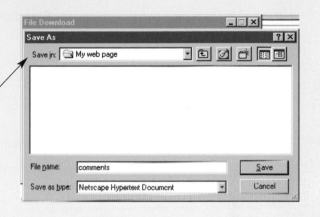

Formatting text, links and the background using body tag

You can view your web page in three different ways: **Normal**, **HTML** and **Preview**. These tabs are shown at the bottom of your web page.

Position your mouse on your web page (**Normal** view), click on the **right** mouse button, select **Page Properties** then **Background**.

You can then set the colour for **Background**, **Text**, **Hyperlink**, and **Visited hyperlink**.

Click on the down arrow next to the item to be formatted, select **More Colours**.

In the **Value** box, enter the colour code or click on the colour required.

Click on **OK**.

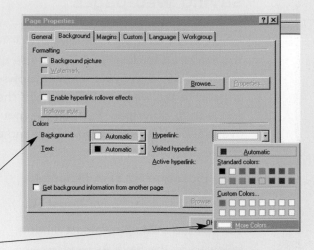

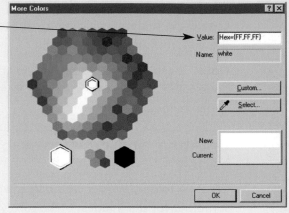

Using standard content

After you have created your first web page you can use the features selected as standard content (eg the background and the colour for text) on other pages you create. If you want to try this out you may use the **first page** web page that is included on the **sample web** folder on the CD that accompanies this book.

Position your mouse on your new web page, click on the **right** mouse button, select **Page Properties**, then **Background**.

Click in **Get background information from another page**.

Click on **Browse**.

Locate the folder with your web page.

Click on the page that has the background information you require.

Click on **OK**.

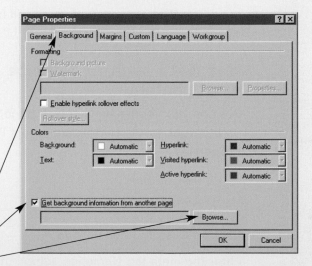

Saving web pages

Click on ▣

Make sure you **Save in:** your web page folder.

Enter the **File name.**

Check the file type is **Web Pages.**

Click on **Save.**

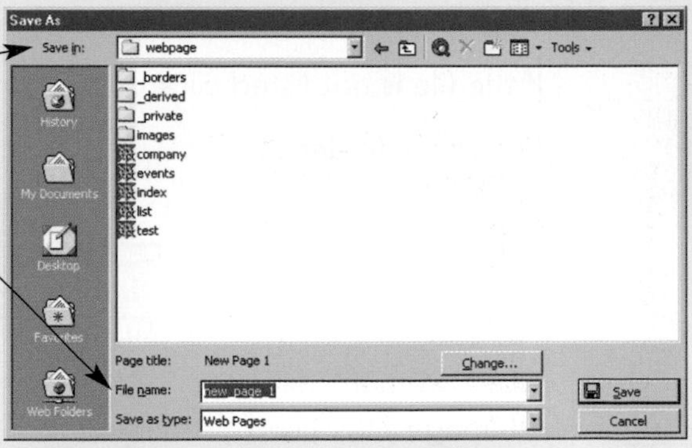

Formatting and using text, images and tables

Inserting text and images

To insert a **text file**, click on **Insert** then select **File.**

In **Files of type:** select **Text Files (*.txt).**

Locate and select the file then click on **Open.**

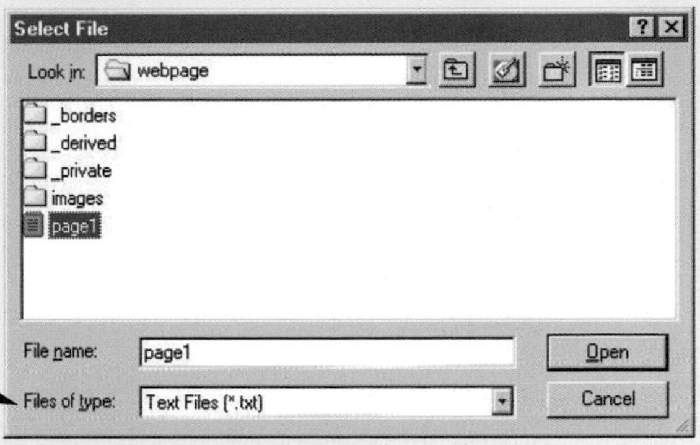

The **Convert Text** window will appear.

Locate and select **Normal paragraphs.**

Click on **OK.**

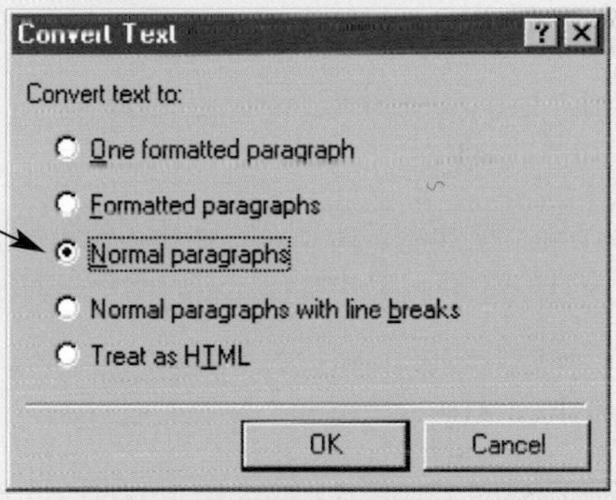

To insert a **picture:**

Click on **Insert, Picture.**

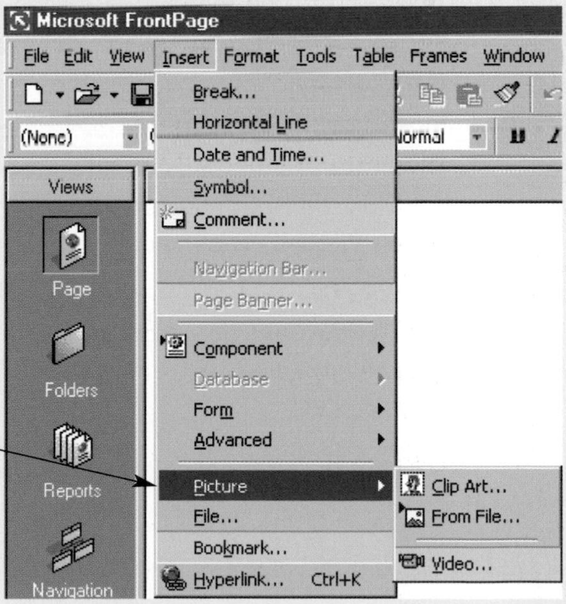

You can select a file or click on **ClipArt**.

If the file is not listed click on

Select the folder to **Look in:**

Select the file.

Click **OK**.

Note: Remember all image files used on web pages must be stored within the web folder in the specified subfolder.

Select File

Look in: images

_vti_cnf	bowl
DELS IMAGES	bronzebut
BGRD	brownbutton
blackbut	burger
bluebutton	burger2
bluebutton2	butbronze2
bluebutton3	chips

File name: chips — OK

Files of type: All Pictures [*.gif;*.jpg;*.png;*.bmp;*.tif;*.wmf;* ▼] — Cancel

OK   Cancel   Clip Art...   Parameters...   Scan...

Picture

Look in: images

Name	Title
DELS IMAGES	
BGRD.gif	images/BGRD.gif
blackbut.jpg	images/blackbut.jpg
bluebutton.gif	images/bluebutton.gif
bluebutton2.jpg	images/bluebutton2.jpg
bluebutton3.jpg	images/bluebutton3.jpg
bowl.gif	images/bowl.gif
bronzebut.gif	images/bronzebut.gif
brownbutton.jpg	images/brownbutton.jpg
burger.gif	images/burger.gif

URL:

OK   Cancel   Clip Art...   Parameters...   Scan...

Setting image attributes

Select the image, click on the **right** mouse button then select **Picture Properties**.

Click on **Appearance**.

Enter the **Properties** required, eg Alignment.

To specify the size click in the Specify size box, then enter the details in the Width and Height boxes.

Click on **OK**.

All images should have **ALT text** (alternative text). This is text that appears when you "hover" over an image when viewing a web page.

To set alternative text:
Select the image.
Click on the **right** mouse button.
Select **Picture Properties**.

Click on **General**
Click in the **Text** box and type the text you wish to appear.
Click on **OK**.

Picture Properties

General | Video | Appearance

Layout

Alignment: Right   Horizontal spacing: 0

Border thickness: 0   Vertical spacing: 0

Size

☑ Specify size   Width: 75   Height: 75
 ⦿ in pixels   ⦿ in pixels
 ○ in percent   ○ in percent

☑ Keep aspect ratio

Picture Properties

General | Video | Appearance

Picture source:
images/frog.gif   Browse...   Edit...

Type
 ⦿ GIF   ☐ Transparent   ○ JPEG   Quality: 75
  ☐ Interlaced   Progressive passes: 0
 ○ PNG

Alternative representations
 Low-Res: Browse...
 Text: Frog image

Default hyperlink
 Location: Browse...
 Target Frame:

Style...

OK   Cancel

Using additional text formatting and special characters

Highlight the text that requires additional formatting. Click on the **right** mouse button and select **Font**.

Click on the required formatting.

Click on **Apply**.

To insert special characters click on **Insert** then **Symbol**.

Click on the required symbol.

Click on **Insert** then **Close**.

Inserting a table

Click on **Table**, then **Insert** and select **Table**.

Enter the details for your table.

Click on **OK**.

Setting table dimensions

Position your mouse on your table. Click on the **right** mouse button then select **Table Properties**.

Select the properties you require.

Click on **OK**.

Note: You now have the option to **Specify height**. This option is not available when you first insert your table.

You may also set the table alignment from this screen.

Setting table or cell alignment

Table alignment can be set in **Table Properties** (see previous section).

To set cell alignment position your mouse on your table, click on the **right** mouse button then select **Cell Properties**.

Select the alignment required.

To specify the width and height click in the **Specify width** and **Specify height** boxes then enter the details.

Make any other changes required.

Click on **OK**.

To create a table for a navigation bar that will appear on all pages click on **Format** and **Shared** borders.

Click in **All Pages**.

Select the area or areas for the border, for example **Left** and **Top**.

Click on **OK**.

Create your table in your border area.

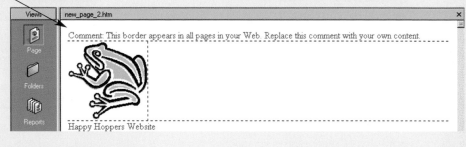

Any items that you wish to be displayed on all pages can be placed in the shared border area.

Formatting and using an interactive form

Setting method and action

To create a form, click on **Insert** and select **Form**, click on **Form**.

When you use a form you will need to select where the information from the form is to be sent and stored, and you may want to send a confirmation message to the person completing the form. This can be done by setting the **method** and **action**.

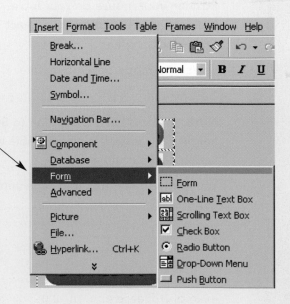

To set method and action **right** mouse click on your form and select **Form Properties**.

Selecting Options and/or Advanced can set up further methods/actions.

Using common input types

From the Insert menu click on **Form** and select the required input type, eg a drop-down menu.

Setting input attributes

Having inserted the form item, ensure that it is selected then **right** mouse click on the field that you have inserted then select **Form Field Properties**.

Add the properties.

In the **Choice** box you can add the first item you wish to appear in the drop-down menu.

Click on **OK**.

Repeat these steps for each item that you wish to appear in the drop-down menu.

You can also select **Validation**.

If you set the validation the person completing the form is required to input data in this item. If they do not a message will appear on the screen informing them that they must select an item. The **Display name** is the name that the user will see to direct them to the information that is required, for example "Please enter a value for **meal**".

Testing a form

Click on **Preview** to test the form.

Linking pages to create a web site

Using images and text as anchors for hyperlinks

Any image or text can be used as an anchor for a hyperlink. Click on the image or highlight the text. Right mouse click, select **Hyperlink...**

Using hyperlinks to an external site

From the **Hyperlink...**

enter the full address in the **URL:** box.

Click on **OK**.

Using hyperlinks to local pages

From the **Hyperlink...** select page to link to.

Click on **OK**.

Using an e-mail link

From the **Hyperlink...** click on

Click on **OK**.

Note: Check the details in the URL: box very carefully as these must be 100% accurate or they will not work. A link that does not work is penalised as a critical error.

Relative links

When linking to pages within your web site it is important to ensure that your links are **relative.** A relative link links to items within the web page folder that has been loaded onto the web. An **absolute** link links to items on your personal disk. If your link is **absolute** it will look for the file on your personal disk. This will not be accessible once your web has been published on the Internet so the link will not work.

Shown below is the HTML code for an absolute link and a relative link. To check your links are relative you can check in the HTML view of your web page.

Relative link: \<p>\<a href="first%20page. htm">Hello\</a>

Absolute link: \<p>\<a href="C:/myweb/first %20page.htm">Hello\</a>

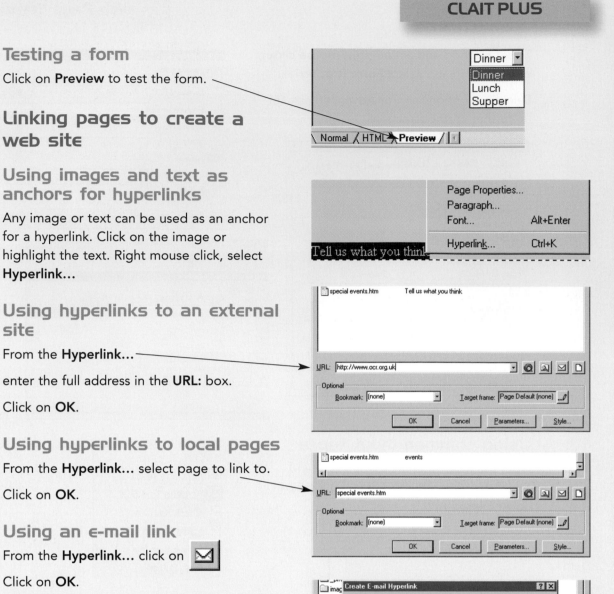

Build Up Exercises

Tasks 1 to 4

Task 1 is designed to allow you to practise some of the skills required to gain the OCR Level 2 Certificate for IT Users (CLAIT PLUS) assessment objectives for Unit 7 Web Page Creation. To cover all the assessment objectives you will have to complete Tasks 2, 3 and 4.

Before you begin

You should know how to:

- create web pages from unformatted source material
- use standard images and formatting to create a consistent house style
- create and format tables and forms
- use meta tags to define content
- set dimensions, alignment and other attributes of page items.

You might want to look at a site that is similar to the one you are going to set up – www.millasmagicalcircus.co.uk

Scenario

You are working for an entertainment company that organises parties and shows for children and adults. The company provides different types of clown and circus acts. The clowns are based in different parts of the country.

The web site's goal is to advertise Creativity's services, make it possible for customers to book on-line, and to encourage customer feedback.

The text and image files for the web site are on the CD that accompanies this book. They are:

bookword	feedback	homepage	package
home	emailus	clowns	booking
maestro	balloons	feedback	saxman
rocky	balls	clownkid	

You may want to look at these files before you begin to get to know the material you will be working with.

You must prepare the web site using the following information:

- The Web Site Map
- The House Style Sheet
- The Standard Content for each page
- The Design Briefs – one for each page

House Style Sheet

Images

- Height and width must be as specified for each image.
- Border must be set to 0 for each image.
- ALT text must be set as specified for each image.

Colour

Background	#FFFFFF	white
Text	#000000	black
Hyperlink	#00FFFF	aqua
Visited Hyperlink	#990099	purple
Active Hyperlink	#FF0000	red

Text styles

Style name	Typeface	Feature	Size	Alignment
Heading	sans serif		18	centre
Subheading	sans serif	bold	12	centre
Body	sans serif		10	left

Tables

Column format:	horizontal alignment	centred
	vertical alignment	middle
Column title format:	horizontal alignment	centred
	vertical alignment	middle

Table text

Style name	Typeface	Feature	Size	Alignment
Column heading	sans serif	bold	12	centre
Package heading	sans serif	bold	12	left
Body	sans serif		10	left

Standard Page Content

The following items must appear on every page of the web site:

Meta tags

Each page must have the following meta tag information:

Name	Value
author	your full name and centre number
keywords	clown, silly clowns, puppets, stilt-walker, circus
description	as specified in the Design Brief for each page

Navigation table

This table of navigation images must be placed at the top of each page:

home.gif	emailus.gif	clowns.gif	booking.gif	feedback.gif

To set the table up:

1   On the **Insert**, **Table** screen, specify:

Size		**Layout**	
Rows	1	Alignment	**centre**
Columns	5	Border size	**0**
		Cellpadding	**0**
		Cellspacing	**0**

2   On the **Table**, **Properties**, **Table** screen, specify:

Width	**480** pixels
Height	**32** pixels

3   On the **Table**, **Properties**, **Cell** screen, specify:

Width	**96** pixels
Height	**32** pixels

Image	ALT text	Hyperlink to
home.gif	home page	index.htm
emailus.gif	e-mail us	e-mail link to info@placeholder.co.uk
clowns.gif	clown acts available	clowns.htm
booking.gif	book online	bookings.htm
feedback.gif	let us know what you think	feedback.htm

Creativity Web Site Map

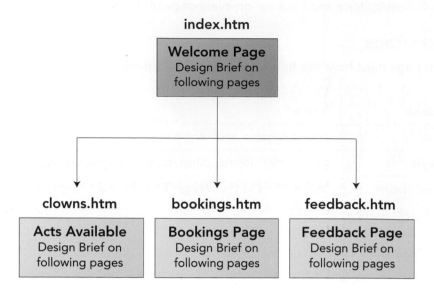

Site structure

- All HTML files for the web site should be contained within the same folder (**unit7**).
- Within **unit7**, there should be a folder called **images**.
- All image files for the web site should be located in the **images** folder.
- All links to files and images on the web site should be **relative** not absolute.

TASK 1

Design Brief for index.htm

What You Have To Do

Assessment Objectives		
1a, 1b	1	Set up a new folder with the name **unit7**. Within this folder, create a new folder and name it **images**. Download the files and images from the CD.
1c, 1f, 2a, 2b, 2d, 2e, 2f, 4a, 4c, 4d, 4e	2	Open FrontPage. Create a new web page and insert the standard content. Include the navigation table – insert the navigation images into the navigation table cells. Insert the **hyperlinks** and the **ALT text** associated with each image.
1d	3	The meta tags should be:

Title: Creativity – for all your clowning needs
Description: Order a Creativity clown for YOUR next function

2a, 2b	4	Insert the image file **maestro** as shown in the layout below, and format as follows:

ALTERNATIVE TEXT   **The Maestro**
ALIGNMENT   **left**
BORDER THICKNESS   **0**
WIDTH   **181**
HEIGHT   **181**

```
+-----------------------------------------------+
|                                               |
|   +---------------------------------------+   |
|   |            Navigation bar             |   |
|   +---------------------------------------+   |
|                                               |
|                                               |
|   +-----------+   We are not magicians ...    |
|   |           |                               |
|   |           |   Organising a ...            |
|   |           |                               |
|   | maestro.gif   Think about ...             |
|   |           |                               |
|   |           |   The Clown People ...        |
|   +-----------+                               |
|                   All types, any time ...     |
|                                               |
|   Booking online ...                          |
|                                               |
|   A good time ...                             |
|                                               |
|   Such a good time ...                        |
|                                               |
+-----------------------------------------------+
```

2a, 2c	5	Insert the text file **homepage.txt** as Normal paragraphs. Ensure that the paragraphs are separated by one clear line space. Apply the house style.
1g	6	Save your web page as **index.htm** in your **unit7** folder. Save the images in the **images** folder.

TASK 2

Design Brief for clowns.htm

What You Have To Do

Assessment Objectives		
lc, lf, 2a, 2b, 2d, 2e, 2f, 4a, 4c, 4d, 4e	1	Create a new web page. Insert the standard content and save as **clowns.htm**.
ld	2	The meta tags should be:

Title: Creativity Packages

Description: These are the basic Creativity clown packages. Custom entertainments are available on request.

Assessment Objectives		
2a, 2d, 2e, 2f	3	Insert the text file **package**, which contains a **table** of booking information, and format as follows:

Table width	**95%**
Cell padding	**3**
Cell spacing	**1**
Border	**1**
Alignment	**centre**

Assessment Objectives		
2b	4	The table contains the images below. Set the alternative text for each image as shown. Do not amend the image width or height.

Image name	Alternative text
balls.gif	Juggler
clownkid.gif	Maxi-Mini
rocky.gif	Mini-Circus
balloons.gif	Balloons

Assessment Objectives		
le, 2a	5	Enter the page heading **Creativity Packages** and apply the house style to the whole document – your page should look like the layout:

<table>
<tr><td colspan="3" align="center">Navigation bar</td></tr>
<tr><td colspan="3" align="center">Creativity Packages</td></tr>
<tr><td></td><td></td><td></td></tr>
<tr><td></td><td></td><td></td></tr>
<tr><td></td><td></td><td></td></tr>
<tr><td></td><td></td><td></td></tr>
<tr><td></td><td></td><td></td></tr>
</table>

Assessment Objectives		
lg	6	Save your work as **clowns.htm** in your **unit7** folder. Save the images in the **images** folder.

TASK 3

Design Brief for bookings.htm

What You Have To Do

Assessment Objectives		
Ic, If, 2a, 2b, 2d, 2e, 2f, 4a, 4c, 4d, 4e	I	Create a new page. Insert the standard content and apply the house style. Save as **bookings.htm**.
Id, Ie	2	The meta tags should be:

Title: Your Creativity Booking

Description: Book a Creativity clown entertainment package for your next family function or business conference.

Ie	3	Set the background colour of the page to pale yellow. The number for the colour is **#FFFFCC**.
2a	4	Insert the text file **bookword.txt**. The **form** should appear as in the layout below.

```
+-------------------------------------------------+
|  +-------------------------------------------+  |
|  |              Navigation bar               |  |
|  +-------------------------------------------+  |
|                                                 |
|            Your Creativity Booking              |
|  +------------------------------------------+   |
|  | Your name: [                           ] |   |
|  | Your e-mail address. [                 ] |   |
|  | Your telephone no: [                   ] |   |
|  |                                          |   |
|  | I would like to book this package: [Balloon▼]|
|  | If you have any special requests, specify here: |
|  | +--------------------------------------+ |   |
|  | |                                      | |   |
|  | |                                      | |   |
|  | |                                      | |   |
|  | +--------------------------------------+ |   |
|  |                                          |   |
|  | [Send Booking] [Clear Form]              |   |
|  | Your booking will be confirmed by email. |   |
|  +------------------------------------------+   |
+-------------------------------------------------+
```

3a	5	Create an interactive form. The form items are as follows:

Start of form	Before the text	**Your name**
End of form	After the line	**Your booking will be …**
Form method	**POST**	
Form action	**http://www.progress-webmail.co.uk/cgi-bin/webmail.cgi**	

Note: This action will automatically process the form information, sending an e-mail to the specified recipient. A thank you page is automatically generated.

What You Have To Do

Assessment Objectives		
3b, 3c	6	Add the following form items:

Type	Name	Field settings
Hidden field	recipient	YOUR e-mail address
Text area	name	40 characters
Text field	e-mail	40 characters
Number	telephone	12 characters
Drop down list	package	Options Juggler Maxi-Mini Mini-circus Balloons
Text area	special	10 lines of 40 characters
Submit button	send booking	VALUE = send booking
Reset button	clear form	VALUE = clear form

3d	7	Test the form to ensure that it correctly sends an e-mail to the recipient.
3b	8	Amend the recipient of the form to be **creativity@placeholder.co.uk**.
1g	9	Save your web page as **bookings.htm** in your **unit7** folder. Save your images in the **images** folder.

TASK 4

Design Brief for feedback.htm

What You Have To Do

Assessment Objectives		
1c, 1f, 2a, 2b, 2d, 2e, 2f, 4a, 4c, 4d, 4e	1	Create a new page. Insert the standard content and apply the house style. Save as **feedback.htm**.
1d, 1e	2	The meta tags should be: Title: Feedback Description: Tell us what you think about us and our web site
1e	3	Insert the image **saxman.jpg** and apply as the page background.

What You Have To Do

2a	4	Insert the text file **feedback.txt**. The **form** should appear as in the layout.

3a	5	Create an interactive form as follows:

Start of form	Before the text	**Your name**
End of form	Before the line	**Click here for Millas Magical Circus**
Form method	**POST**	
Form action	http://www.progress-webmail.co.uk/cgi-bin/webmail.cgi	

3b 3c	6	Add the following form items:

Type	Name	Field settings
Text area	name	20 characters
Text field	e-mail	20 characters
Drop down list	choice	Options Outstanding Very Good Good Average Below Average One of the best that I've visited
Drop down list	age	Options 21 or under 22–39 40–59 60 plus
Submit button	send booking	VALUE = Send to Creativity
Reset button	clear form	VALUE = Forget it!

What You Have To Do

Assessment Objectives		
4a, 4b	7	Add an external link to the text: **Click here for Millas Magical Circus** The link reference is **http://www.millasmagicalcircus.co.uk**
3d	8	Test the form to ensure that it correctly sends an e-mail to the recipient.
1g	9	Save your web page as **feedback.htm** in your **unit7** folder. Save your images in the **images** folder.
4e	10	Test that all the web site links work. Close your work and the program.

UNIT 8 Electronic Communication

This unit is designed to test your ability to use e-mail and personal information management (PIM) software to receive, transmit messages and attachments electronically and to set diary entries, call meetings, and organise folders.

You may find it easier to undertake this unit if you have completed the Electronic Communication unit at Level 1. If you have done so, you will already know how to:

- identify and use e-mail and browsing software
- transmit and receive e-mail messages and attachments
- navigate the World Wide Web
- use search techniques to locate data on the Web
- manage and print electronic documents.

To pass this unit

You must complete the three-hour OCR-set assignment without making any critical errors, and with no more than three accuracy errors. If you do not achieve a Pass you may re-take the assessment using a different assignment.

You cannot claim both Unit 8 Electronic Communication and Unit 21 Electronic Communication (Microsoft Office Specialist Outlook Core) towards the three optional units of the Level 2 qualification, due to an overlap in content.

Your work will be marked by your tutor, and externally moderated by OCR.

Critical errors

- Failure to show all specified files attached to e-mail.
- E-mail address is missing or incorrect.
- Calendar entries are incorrect day and/or time.
- Failure to enter calendar entries or schedule meetings as specified.

Accuracy errors

- Each instance of an error in entering data. In this unit apply one data entry error for any error(s) in a subject heading, the content of e-mail message, the details in a calendar entry, a 'to do' task entry, the content of a note.
- Each instance of an error in completing an assessment objective.

What will you learn?

When you have completed this unit you should be able to:

- use advanced e-mail features to co-ordinate information
- set up distribution lists and use address book
- use PIM software to organise schedules and business data
- manage mailbox and folders
- publish/print calendar dates.

How to meet the assessment objectives

You will be introduced to **one** method of achieving the assessment objectives. There will be other methods of carrying out these tasks. Only objectives that were not covered in Level 1 are included.

You will already know how to use e-mail and browsing software, transmit and receive e-mail messages and attachments, navigate the World Wide Web, use search techniques to locate data on the Web, manage and print electronic documents.

Now we will deal with the new areas.

Copying a message to other people ensuring confidentiality of addresses

Having entered your e-mail message, check that the ⎡Bcc ->⎤ box is displayed at the top of your message.

If it is not displayed, go to **View**, then click on **Bcc**. You can then enter the e-mail address of the recipient in the Bcc box.

If you have previously stored the address of the recipient, click on ⎡Bcc ->⎤ then select the name(s) of the people or groups you wish to receive the message. Click on ⎡Bcc ->⎤ and the name(s) will move to the **Bcc** box.

Click **OK**.

Prioritising outgoing mail messages

On the top toolbar click on ⎡❗⎤ to prioritise your message.

Creating an e-mail signature

From your Inbox go to **Tools, Options, Mail Format**. Select then click on **Signature Picker, New**.

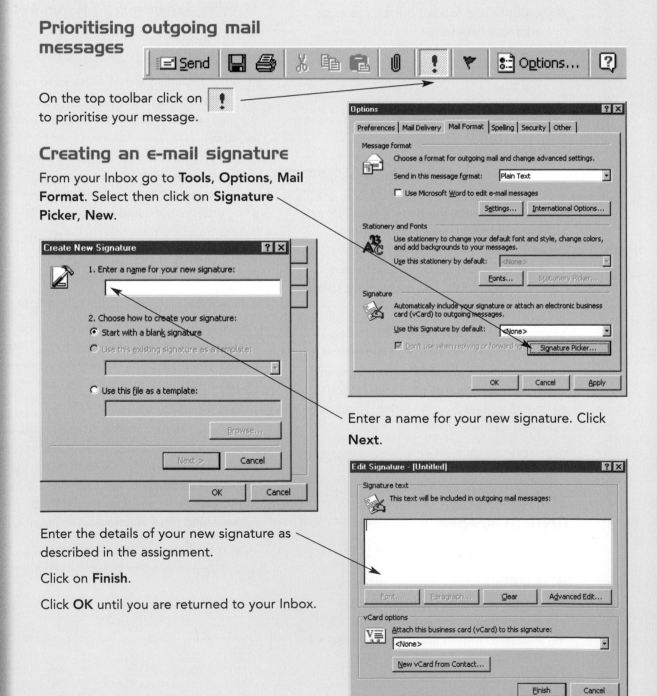

Enter a name for your new signature. Click **Next**.

Enter the details of your new signature as described in the assignment.

Click on **Finish**.

Click **OK** until you are returned to your Inbox.

Adding an e-mail signature to outgoing messages

Click **Tools** then **Options** from the **Mail Format** menu. In the **Signature section** click on the down arrow next to **Use this signature by default**.

Select the signature you have created. Click on **OK**.

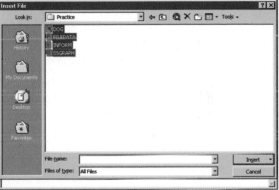

Attaching multiple files to an e-mail message

Enter a message. Click on the **insert file** icon.

Find the files you wish to insert. Hold down the **Shift** key and click on each file in turn.

Click on **Insert**.

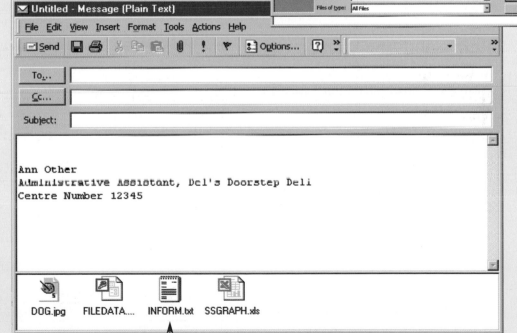

Check your files have been inserted.

Addressing out-going mail messages

Click in the **To ...** box and enter the e-mail address. Check the accuracy of all e-mail addresses *very* carefully as any error is penalised as a **critical error**.

Using an address book

Creating a group or a distribution list of contacts

From the **Tools** menu, select **Address Book**. Click on **New** then select **New Group**.

Enter the group name.

Click on **Select Members** to add names from your address book.

or

Enter the name and e-mail address of the first member then click **Add**. When you have added all the members click **OK**.

If you are adding members from your address book, hold down the Shift key and click on each of the names (or groups) you wish to add, then click **Select**.

The name will be listed under **Members:** Click **OK**, then **OK** again, to close the address book.

Retrieving and using stored e-mail addresses

From the **Inbox** click on the 📧 New ▾ icon on the toolbar.

On the new message click on **To...**

Click on the name or names of the recipient(s) then click on **To ->**

Click **OK**.

Retrieve and use stored distribution list as specified

Follow the steps for retrieving and using stored e-mail addresses above. Click on the group name for the recipients.

You will notice that the icon for a group or list is different from an individual entry.

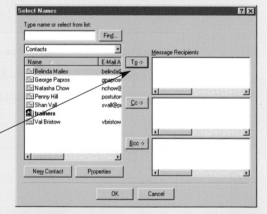

Creating notes

On the **Outlook Shortcuts** menu bar click on

On the toolbar click **New**.

Enter the details.

Then click on ☒

Creating to-do tasks

On the **Outlook Shortcuts** menu bar click on

Click and enter task.

Press return to add to the list.

Use personal information manager software to access, enter and amend information

Accessing calendar entries

On the **Outlook Shortcuts** menu bar click on ⟶

Creating calendar entries

From **Calendar** click on the date for your entry.

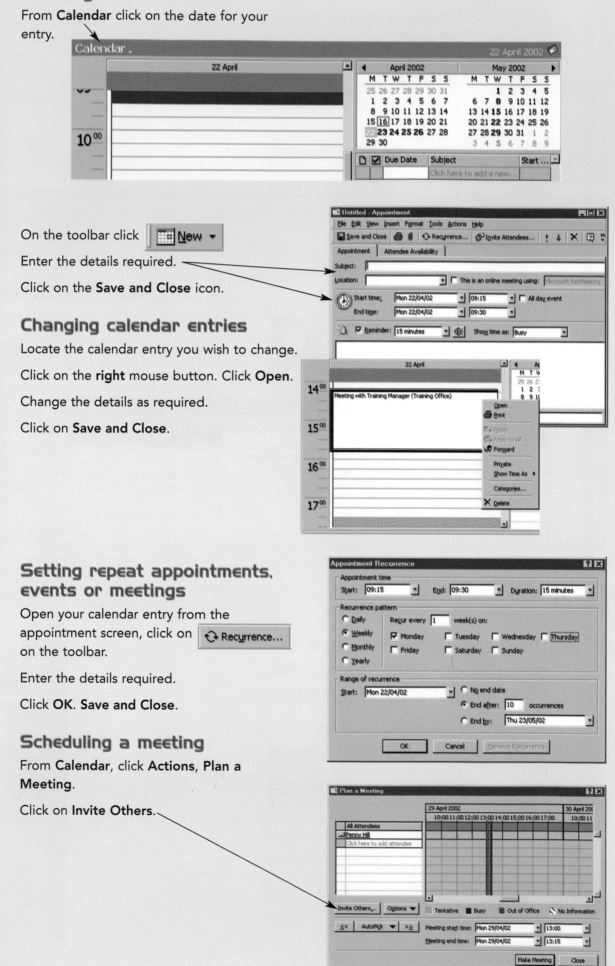

On the toolbar click | New ▾ |

Enter the details required.

Click on the **Save and Close** icon.

Changing calendar entries

Locate the calendar entry you wish to change.

Click on the **right** mouse button. Click **Open**.

Change the details as required.

Click on **Save and Close**.

Setting repeat appointments, events or meetings

Open your calendar entry from the appointment screen, click on | ↻ Recurrence... | on the toolbar.

Enter the details required.

Click **OK**. **Save and Close**.

Scheduling a meeting

From **Calendar**, click **Actions**, **Plan a Meeting**.

Click on **Invite Others**.

Type or click on the name(s) of the individual or group(s) you wish to invite to the meeting.

Click on **Required ->**

After each selection the names will appear in the box under **Message Recipients:**

Click on **OK**.

You will now return to the **Plan a Meeting** window. Click on **Make Meeting.**

You will be returned to the meetings window. Enter the details, ie subject, location, start and end time.

Click on **Send** then **Close** the Plan a Meeting window.

Adjusting your work day or week

From **Calendar**, click **Tools**, **Options** **Preferences**, then **Calendar Options.**

Set your work day/week as required.

Click **OK.**

Setting the alarm

Double-click on the entry to which you want to add an alarm. From the **Appointment** window, click in the box next to **Reminder**. A tick should appear in the box.

Click on the down arrow at the end of the box showing the time.

Select the number of hours or minutes for the alarm.

Click **Save and Close**.

Using notes to hold file contents

Select the file you want to hold in **notes**.

Click on the **right** mouse button, click **Open**.

Press **Ctrl+A** to select the entire file.

From the **Edit** menu click **Copy**.

Click on **New** to open a new note.

Click on the note and press **Ctrl+V**. The contents of the file will be copied.

To close the note click on ✖

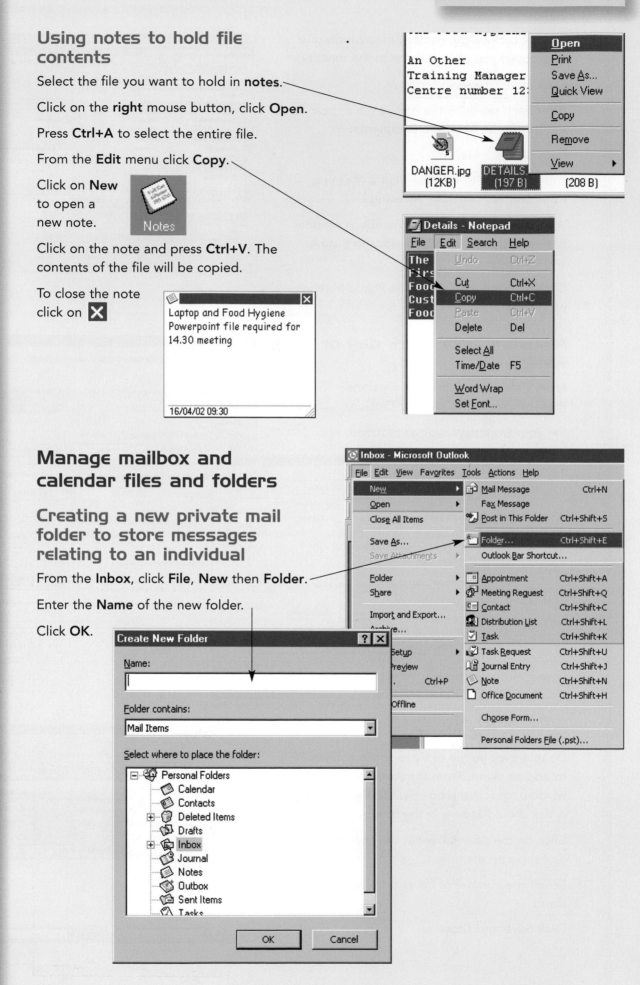

Manage mailbox and calendar files and folders

Creating a new private mail folder to store messages relating to an individual

From the **Inbox**, click **File**, **New** then **Folder**.

Enter the **Name** of the new folder.

Click **OK**.

Moving messages between folders

Select the message to be moved. Click on the **right** mouse button.

Click on **Move to Folder**.

Click on the folder to which the message is to be moved.

Click **OK**.

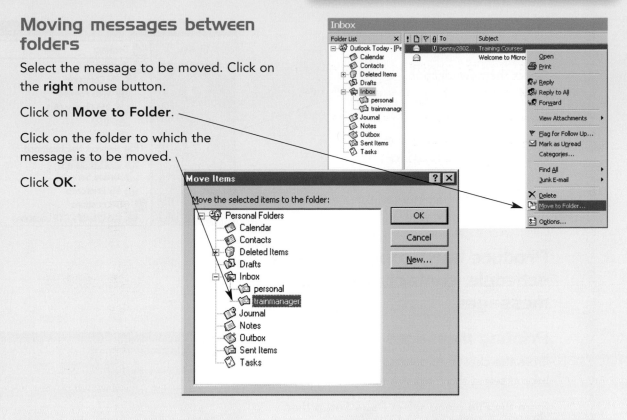

Deleting calendar entries

From Calendar, locate the entry you wish to delete.

Position your mouse on the entry.

Click on the **right** mouse button. Click **Delete**.

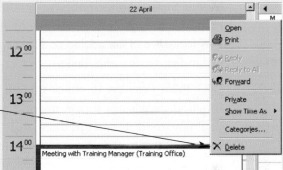

Storing an attachment outside the mailbox structure

Open the message that contains the attachment.

Click **File, Save Attachments**.

Ensure that each of the files you wish to store is highlighted.

Click **OK**.

139

Select the new location.

Click on **OK**, close the message.

Using an attachment in another application

Once you have stored your attachments outside the mailbox you can open and use them in the normal way.

Produce hard copy of weekly schedule, contact details and messages

Printing messages

From the chosen folder (eg **Sent Items**, **Inbox**) select the message you wish to print.

From the **File** menu select **Page Setup** then **Memo Style**. Adjustments/selections can be made from **Page Setup**, for example headers and footers can be added to **Messages**, **Calendar**, **Notes** and **Tasks**.

Click **Print Preview** to check that **all** the required details are shown on your printouts. You may need to change the margin settings for some items, or select an alternative **Layout** (eg Portrait or Landscape).

Click **Print** then **OK**.

Selecting **Table Style** instead of **Memo Style** from the **Page Setup** menu will print a list of the contents of the selected folder.

Printing the calendar or schedule

From **Calendar**, click on **File**, select **Print**.

Select the **Print Style** required, generally this will be **Weekly Style**.

Select the **Start** and **End** date

Check **Preview** before printing.

Click on **Print**.

You will be returned to the Print menu, click **OK**.

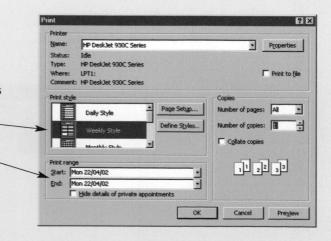

Printing contact details

From the **Outlook Shortcuts** menu select
Contacts, click on **File,** select **Page Setup**.

Select the **Style** from the options given,
usually **Card Style**. Click **Print** then **OK**.

Printing notes

From **Notes,** click **Edit, Select All**.

Click **File, Print**.

Click in the box to select
the **Print Options**
(if specified).

Click on **OK**.

Printing to-do tasks

From **Tasks,** click **File, Page Setup**.

Click on the **Style** you require, usually **Memo
Style**.

The **Page Setup: Memo Style** window will
appear. Add the details you require (eg
headers and footers).

Click **Print**.

You will be returned to the **Print** window.
Click **OK**.

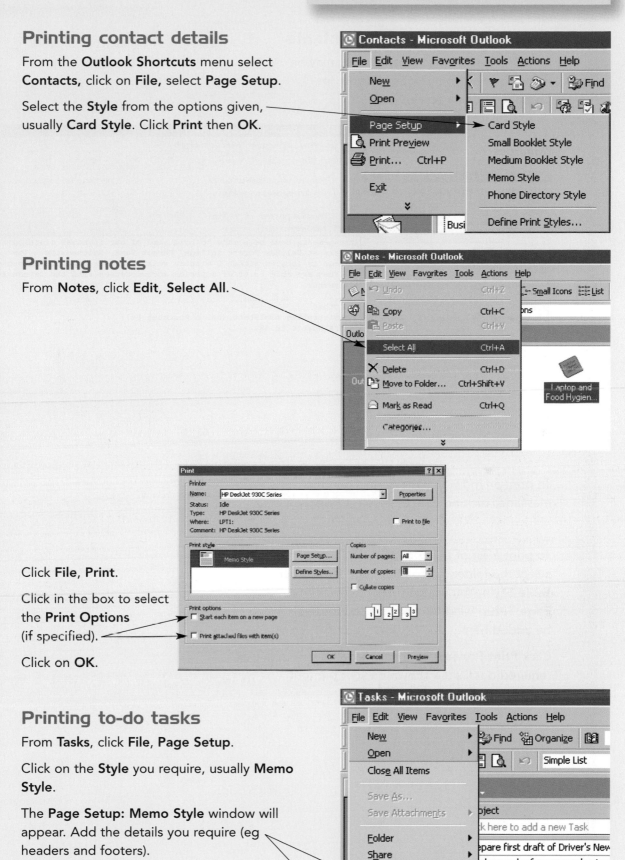

Printing e-mail folder contents

Read the instructions **carefully**. You may be asked to print from the **Sent Items**, in **Compose** or as a **screen print**.

Sent

Compose

To print an individual message, open the message, click on **File**, then select **Print**.

To print a list of the contents of a folder, select the folder, go to **File, Page Setup** then **Table Style**. You will be presented with the **Page Setup** window. Headers and footers can be added here.

Click **Print Preview** to check that **all** the required details are shown on your printout. Click **Print** then **OK**.

Build Up Exercises

TASK 1

This task is designed to allow you to practise some of the skills required to gain the OCR Level 2 Certificate for IT Users (CLAIT PLUS) assessment objectives for Unit 8 Electronic Communication. To cover all the assessment objectives you will have to complete Tasks 2 and 3.

Before you begin

You should know how to:

- organise schedules and business data
- print calendar dates.

Scenario

You are working for Anna Labadie, the Managing Director of Creativity, an entertainment company that organises parties and shows. It has been agreed that a regional structure should be put in place, with the following responsibilities:

Northern	Mike Brook
Central	Mary Edwards
Southern	Jael Meyer

Your first task is to set up your calendar, and schedule your meetings and appointments.

What You Have To Do

Assessment Objectives		
3b, 3d, 3f, 3h, 3i	1	Set up your calendar so that the working day starts at **8.30**, ends at **17.00**, and has **30 minute** time slots. Your working week runs **Monday** to **Friday**.

Schedule the following meetings and appointments for next week.

Monday	Time	9.30
	Duration	2.5 hours
	Location	Victoria Hotel, Chester
	Appointment	Auditions
	Set the appointment to recur every week	

Tuesday	Time	9.30
	Duration	1.5 hours
	Location	Chester – factory site
	Appointment	Meeting with new suppliers – Jackson Brown
	Time	16.00
	Duration	1 hour
	Location	John Davis Associates – Bridge Street
	Appointment	Meeting with John to finalise new ad artwork
	To do task	Prepare mailing for annual meeting by Wed

What You Have To Do

Wednesday Time   11.15

            Duration   45 minutes

            Location   Joan Green's Workshop

            Appointment   Meeting with Joan Green to agree new costume designs and costs

                                    Ensure that you set a reminder or alarm 45 minutes before the meeting to allow time to travel

            To do task   Send cost estimates to Jael Meyer today

Thursday   Travel to York – out of office all day Hayton Hotel, York

Friday   Time   9.15

            Duration   1 hour

            Location   Hotel Reception

            Appointment   Meet with Tony Thomas, Nadine Henschel and Denise Hart to sign new contracts

            Time   11.45

            Duration   30 minutes

            Location   York Theatre

            Appointment   Manager – to obtain revue costings

            To do task   Arrange payment to Theatre

Print a copy of your diary for Anna Labadie for this week so that she can arrange further appointments around your existing schedule.

Ensure all calendar entries are shown in full. Include your name on the printout.

TASK 2

Notes

- In order to complete this assignment your tutor will have to send you this e-mail. It must be prepared and sent to you before you start. Capitalisation should be as shown:

Subject:	Auditions
Message:	Please note that the weekly auditions will now take place at 9.30 am every Tuesday, in the Ballroom of the Victoria Hotel, Chester.
	I need at least one of the regionals with me each week. Please ask them to indicate availability on the attached file (avail.csv) and return it to you so that you can complete the schedule.
	You will also find a copy of the animation for the web advertising, and the text for the new presentations. Please ask the regionals for comments by Friday.
Signature:	Anna Labadie CREATIVITY
Attachments:	prestext.txt avail.csv clownad.gif

- You will need an e-mail address from which to open the e-mail and send a reply.
- You will need the files **prestext**, **avail** and **clownad** to attach to an e-mail that you will send.
- To complete the assignment you will need on-line access to e-mail. Although the e-mails are not read or assessed in any way, you **must** use the following e-mail addresses:

alabadie@progress-media.co.uk
mbrook@progress-media.co.uk
medwards@progress-media.co.uk
jmeyer@progress-media.co.uk

- You should also note that company policy for the use of e-mail states that:

  - all incoming e-mail messages must be stored in a dedicated archive folder and then deleted from the Inbox
  - all outgoing messages must be saved and printed showing header details, including sender, recipient(s), date and subject
  - all outgoing messages must be sent with the default priority set to normal (except where otherwise specified)
  - all outgoing messages must close with your company approved e-mail signature in the form:

    Your full name
    CREATIVITY
    Centre number

Before you begin

You should know how to:

- set up distribution lists and use address book
- manage your mailbox and folders
- print e-mails.

Scenario

You are now going to set up a distribution list and exchange e-mails.

What You Have To Do

Assessment Objectives		
2a	1	Details of the regional co-ordinators should be added to your contacts list.

SURNAME	BROOK
FIRST NAME	MIKE
REGION	NORTHERN
E-MAIL	mbrook@progress-media.co.uk

SURNAME	EDWARDS
FIRST NAME	MARY
REGION	CENTRAL
E-MAIL	medwards@progress-media.co.uk

SURNAME	MEYER
FIRST NAME	JAEL
REGION	SOUTHERN
E-MAIL	jmeyer@progress-media.co.uk

AO	#	Task
2b	2	Create an e-mail distribution list named **regions** holding the e-mail addresses of these contacts.
1e	3	Create and store your company approved e-mail signature.
4a	4	Configure your e-mail system to ensure that a dedicated archive folder is created to hold messages from the Managing Director (Anna Labadie). Call this folder **mdlabadie**.
2a, 4b, 4d	5	Anna Labadie has sent you an e-mail message concerning Auditions. Read the message entitled **Auditions**. Store the attached files outside the mailbox structure. The files are: **prestext**, **avail** and **clownad** Add Anna Labadie's address to your address storage facility. Archive the message following the company policy.
3c, 3j, 4e	6	You need the file **prestext** to complete your work on the presentation, copy the file to your Notes pages.

What You Have To Do

Assessment Objectives		
Ia, Ib, Id, If, Ig, Ih, 2c, 2d	7	Prepare the following message for the regionals:

Subject	Auditions
Message text	Please note that the weekly auditions will now take place at 9.30 am every Tuesday, in the Ballroom of the Victoria Hotel, Chester.
	Anna needs at least one of you with her each week. Please indicate availability on the attached file (avail.csv) and return it to me so that I can complete the schedule.
	You will also find a copy of the animation for the web advertising, and the text for the new presentations. Please let Anna have any comments by Friday.

Attach a copy of the files that you received with the **Auditions** message:

prestext, **avail** and **clownad**

Ensure that a copy of your message is delivered to Anna Labadie for information.

Mark the message as High Priority, and ensuring your system saves outgoing messages, send the e-mail.

5a	8	Print **one** copy of the e-mail message you have sent.
5c	9	Print a copy of your contacts list showing Surname, First Name and full e-mail address for each contact using a small card style – ie many contacts presented on one page.

TASK 3

Before you begin

You should know how to:

- use advanced e-mail features to co-ordinate information
- print Notes pages using memo style
- print To-do tasks using memo style
- print a list of the contents of an e-mail folder.

Due to the change in the Audition times, it will be necessary to amend your calendar entries. You have also been asked to arrange for Jael Meyer to attend the meeting with the manager of the York Theatre on Friday.

What You Have To Do

Assessment Objectives		
3g	1	Schedule this meeting with Jael Meyer:

Friday Time 10.15
Duration 1 hour
Subject To discuss costings
Location Hayton Hotel, York

3c	2	Create the following note:

Meet Jael Meyer for pre-meeting discussion – take details of costs and income from last year.

1a, 1c, 1f, 1h, 2c	3	Prepare a message to Jael Meyer, using the following information.

Recipient jmeyer@progress-media.co.uk

Subject COSTINGS MEETING

Message text We need to discuss the costings before the meeting with the manager of the theatre.

If you need overnight accommodation let me know, and I can arrange it.

Copy the message to Mike Brook and Mary Edwards ensuring confidentiality of addresses.

Send the e-mail.

5a	4	Produce a screen print of the e-mail message from the **COMPOSE MODE** making sure that the confidential recipients are shown.
3a, 3e, 4c	5	Amend your calendar entries to reflect the changes to your schedule –

- Remove the Auditions meeting on Monday and reschedule it to Tuesday – same time, duration, location, and recurring each week
- Remove the meeting with Jackson Brown on Tuesday at 9.30, and reschedule it for Monday at 14.00 – same duration and location

5d	6	Print one copy of your Notes pages using memo style.
5e	7	Print one copy of your To-do tasks list using a memo style.
5b	8	Since you have made changes to your schedule, you should print **one** copy of your revised calendar using the weekly style.
5f	9	Print a list of contents of the e-mail folder **mdlabadie**.
	10	Exit using the correct procedures.

UNIT 9 Graphs and Charts

This unit is designed to test your ability to use spreadsheet software to solve problems by creating graphs and charts. You will gain an understanding of the purpose of presenting data in different formats.

You may find it easier to undertake this unit if you have completed the Graphs and Charts and the Spreadsheets units at Level 1. If you have done so, you will already know how to:

- use spreadsheet software
- use an input device to enter and edit data accurately
- insert, replicate and format arithmetical formulae
- use common numerical formatting and alignment
- manage and print spreadsheet documents
- produce pie charts, line graphs and bar/column charts
- select and present single and comparative sets of data
- set numerical parameters and format data
- manage and print graph and chart documents

To pass this unit

You must complete the three-hour OCR-set assignment without making any critical errors, and with no more than three accuracy errors. If you do not achieve a Pass you may re-take the assessment using a different assignment.

Your work will be marked by your tutor, and externally moderated by OCR.

Critical errors

- A missing or incorrect value on pie chart.
- A missing or incorrect value on bar/column chart.
- A missing or incorrect value on line-column graph.
- A missing or incorrect value on XY scatter graph.
- A legend where the details cannot be identified.
- Labels that do not identify data.
- A missing axis title.
- Failure to select the specified graph/chart type (pie, bar/column, line-column, or XY scatter).

Accuracy errors

- Each instance of an error in entering data. In this unit apply one data entry error for any error(s) in a title, an axis label, a data label or a legend label.
- Each instance of an error in completing an assessment objective.

What will you learn?

When you have completed this unit you should be able to:

- select and control source data
- present data using graphs and charts
- format axis and labels
- format the presentation of graphs and charts
- use graphs to extrapolate information to predict future values.

How to meet the assessment objectives

You will be introduced to **one** method of achieving the assessment objectives. There will be other methods of carrying out these tasks. Only objectives that were not covered in Level 1 are included.

You will already know how to use spreadsheets, how to produce pie charts, line graphs, bar and column charts. You will have selected and presented single, comparative and subsets of data, set numerical parameters, formatted data, and printed graph and chart documents

Now we will deal with the new areas.

Presenting data

Using an exploded pie chart

Select your data.

Click the **Chart Wizard** icon.

Click the **Pie** icon.

Click the **Exploded Pie** icon.

You can now look at your data in this style.

Enter the information requested by the wizard to complete the chart.

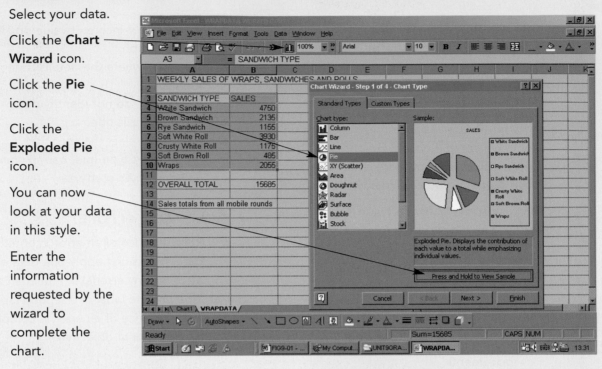

Emphasising a pie chart segment

To pull out one slice of a pie chart:

Select the slice you want to move.

Drag away from the centre of the chart to the required position.

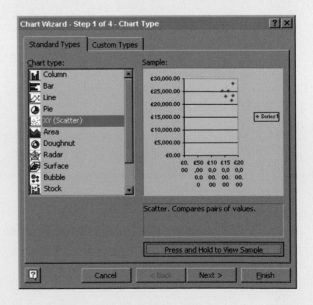

Using an XY scatter graph

Select your data.

Click the **Chart Wizard** icon.

Click the XY (Scatter) icon.

Enter the information requested by the wizard to complete the chart.

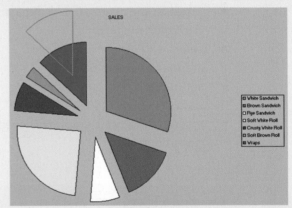

Setting parameters

Selecting and displaying data labels

To display data labels on a chart:

Select the data.

Click the **Chart Wizard** icon.

Click the **Column** icon.

When you reach Step 3 of 4 of the wizard, click **Show value**.

Enter the information requested by the wizard to complete the chart.

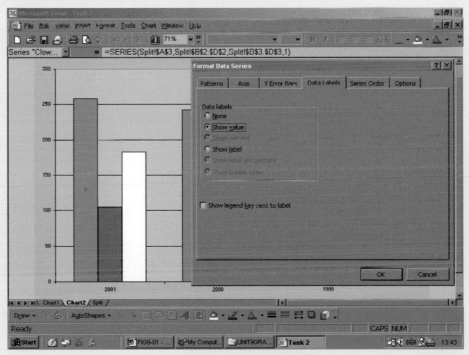

Adding data labels

To add data labels to an existing data series:

Click on the series.

The **Format Data Series** screen appears.

Click **Show value**.

Click **OK**.

Applying a legend

To display a legend on a chart:

Select the data.

Click the **Chart Wizard** icon.

Use any chart type – this example is **line**.

When you reach Step 3 of 4 of the wizard, click **Legend**, **Show legend**.

Enter the information requested by the wizard to complete the chart.

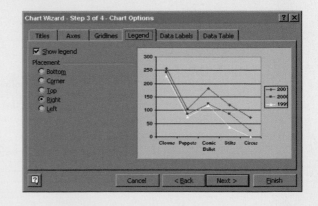

Adding a legend

Click the chart on which you want to add a legend.

Click **Chart, Chart Options, Legend**.

Click on the **Show legend** check box.

Under **Placement**, click your chosen option.

Click **OK**.

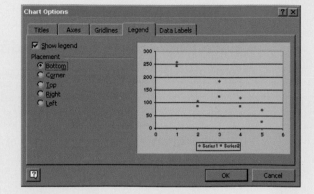

Setting the upper and lower limits and the intervals on axes

Move your mouse to the axis you want to change until you see the Value Axis label appear.

Double-click.

The **Format Axis** screen will appear. On the **Scale** tab you can change the values for:

Minimum
Maximum
Major unit
Minor unit

When you have made your changes, click **OK**.

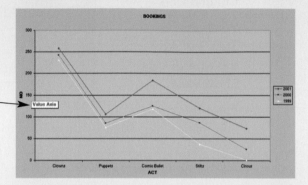

Inserting a trendline

Move your mouse to the data series to which you want to add a trendline.

Click **Chart, Add Trendline, Type**.

Click the type of line you want.

Click **OK**.

The line will be placed on your chart.

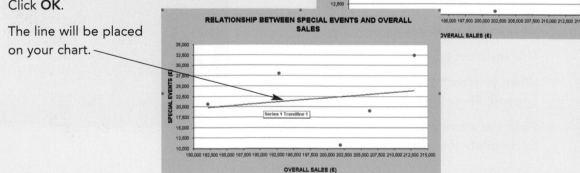

Inserting a trendline equation

Move your mouse to the trendline for which you want to display an equation.

Click **Format, Selected Trendline, Options**.

Click the **Display equation on chart** box.

Click **OK**.

The equation will then be displayed on the chart.

You can move the box to your chosen position.

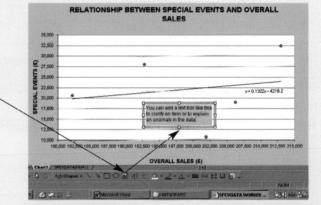

Inserting a textbox

Select the text box icon ▣ on the Drawing toolbar.

Move to your chart and drag the box to your chosen size.

You can enter text in the box.

You can move the box to any position.

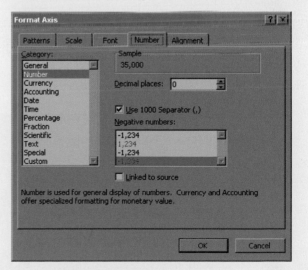

Formatting

Applying specific numeric formatting on axes

Double-click on the axis on which you want to make the changes.

The **Format Axis** screen will appear.

Click **Number** tab.

Select required format.

Click **OK**.

Applying or removing background fill to the plot area

Move your mouse on the chart you want to change until you see the **Plot Area** label appear.

Double-click.

The **Format Plot Area** screen will appear.

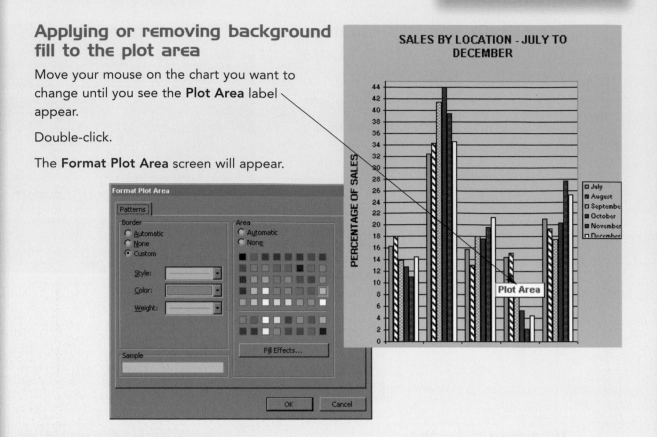

You can make changes as required by clicking on the relevant points, or selecting the options for both the area and the border.

When you have made all your changes, click **OK**.

Applying fill to bars in a data series

Double-click on the data series on which you want to apply or change the fill.

The **Format Data Series** screen will appear.

Click the **Patterns** tab.

Select the **Area** colour or **Fill Effect** that you require.

Click **OK**.

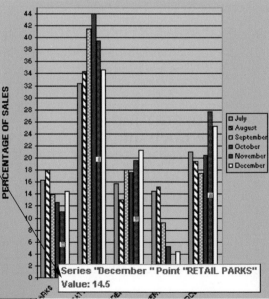

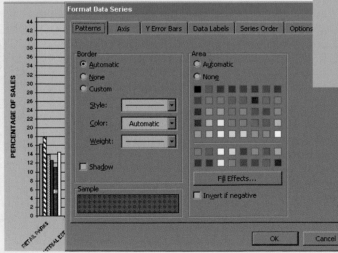

Setting the style and weight of lines and markers

Double-click on the line on which you want to apply or change the style or weight. You can do this in the legend.

The **Format Legend Key** screen will appear.

Click the **Pattern** tab.

You can now change both the line and the marker:

Line   Style
            Colour
            Weight

Marker Style
            Foreground colour
            Background colour
            Size

Make the changes that you require.

Click **OK**.

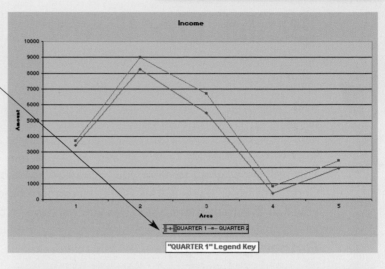

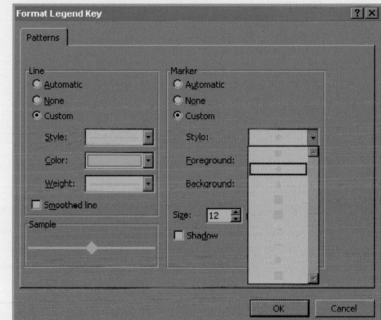

Printing

Printing graphs in landscape or portrait

Click **File**, **Page Setup**.

Select **Portrait** or **Landscape** as required by clicking on the relevant box.

Click **OK**.

Build Up Exercises

This task is designed to allow you to practise some of the skills required to gain the OCR Level 2 Certificate for IT Users (CLAIT PLUS) assessment objectives for Unit 9 Graphs and Charts. To cover all the assessment objectives you will have to complete Tasks 2, 3, and 4.

Before you begin

You should know how to:

- select and control source data
- present data using graphs and charts
- format axis and labels
- format the presentation of graphs and charts.

NOTES: You will use only two data files for Tasks 1 to 4.

These files are limited in size so that you can better see and understand the results of your work.

When you carry out the OCR assessment (and the practice assignment on the CD) each graph that you produce will be drawn from a different file and some of those files will be larger. You will also be required to do more formatting.

Scenario

Creativity is a company that provides different types of clown and circus-style acts to entertain at functions and children's parties. The clowns and variety acts are freelance and are employed on a per function basis. They are based in different parts of the country.

The company has been expanding. You have been asked to produce reports to review past successes and plan future expansion.

You will need to use two data files, **split** and **ttlbooks**, to produce the reports. You will find them on the CD that accompanies this book.

You must prepare the graphs and charts according to the company House Style Sheet.

House Style Sheet

Pie charts

Style name	Typeface	Point size	Feature
Title	serif	16	bold
Data labels	sans serif	10	
Legend	sans serif	10	
Number format	sans serif	10	0 decimal places

Bar or column charts, line graphs, XY scatter graphs

Style name	Typeface	Point size	Feature
Title	serif	16	bold
x axis title	sans serif	10	bold and italic
y axis title	sans serif	10	bold and italic
Legend	sans serif	10	
x axis text and numbering	sans serif	10	
y axis text and numbering	sans serif	10	
Number format	sans serif	10	0 decimal places
Text box	sans serif	8	
Trendline equation	sans serif	8	
Trendline			solid, thin, black
Markers		8	solid diamonds – black

Typeface

Please use just **one** serif and **one** sans serif font. Use the same fonts on Tasks 1 to 4.

Plot area

All charts must be presented with the plot area **WHITE**.

Headers and footers

All charts must include your **name**, **centre number**, the **filename** and the **date** in the **footer**.

Prepare a report showing the relative popularity of the acts in 2001.

What You Have To Do

Assessment Objectives		
Ia	1	Open the file **split**. Save it using your program's file type. The data shows the number of bookings for each type of act from 1996 to 2001. Note that some of the acts were not introduced until later years, and show zeroes in years before their introduction.
Ib, 2a	2	Create an **exploded pie** chart to display the number of bookings for each act (Clowns, Puppets, Comic Ballet, Stilts, and Circus) in **2001**.
3a	3	Use the title: **BOOKINGS – 2001**
3b	4	Display the **label and percentage** for each pie slice, ensuring that each of the values can be read clearly.
3c	5	Apply a colour or effect to each **pie slice**. Each should be different in appearance **when printed**. Do *not* use a legend on this chart.
2b	6	You are particularly interested in the number of times the Puppets were booked during 2001.
		Make the **Puppets** pie slice stand out by pulling it away from the rest of the chart.
4a, 4c, 4d	7	Apply the house style.
	8	Save the chart.
5b	9	Print your pie chart in **portrait** orientation.

TASK

Prepare a report showing the bookings for all the acts from 1996 to 2001.

What You Have To Do

Assessment Objectives		
Ia	1	Open the file **split**. Save it using your program's file type.
Ic, 2c	2	Create a **bar** chart to display the number of bookings for each act (Clowns, Puppets, Comic Ballet, Stilts, and Circus) in all years from **1996** to **2001**.
3a	3	Use the title: **BOOKINGS 1996–2001** Use the x axis title: **YEAR** Use the y axis title: **NUMBER**
3c	4	Display the series in a legend. The x axis labels should be 1996 to 2001.

What You Have To Do

Assessment Objectives		
3d	5	Format the **y axis** as follows: Minimum value: **0** Maximum value: **280** Interval: **40**
4e	6	Apply a different fill effect to each of the series (Clowns, Puppets, Comic Ballet, Stilts, and Circus) to ensure that each one is distinctive in appearance **when printed**. Make sure that the legend clearly reflects these differences.
4a, 4c, 4d	7	Apply the house style.
	8	Save the chart.
5a	9	Print your bar chart in **landscape** orientation.

TASK 3

Before you begin

You should know how to:

- use graphs to extrapolate information to predict future values.

Prepare a report showing the relationship between the bookings for the southern region and total bookings for 2001 and 2002.

What You Have To Do

Assessment Objectives		
1a	1	Open the file **ttlbooks**. Save it using your program's file type.
1d, 1e, 2e	2	Create an **XY scatter** graph to plot the relationship between the data for the **SOUTH** and the **PERIOD TOTAL** for the year 2002.
3a	3	Use the title: **COMPARATIVE FIGURES 2002** Use the x axis title: **SOUTH (£)** Use the y axis title: **PERIOD TOTAL (£)**
3d	4	Format the **x axis** as follows: Minimum value: **0** Maximum value: **15000** Interval: **2500**
3d	5	Format the **y axis** as follows: Minimum value: **10000** Maximum value: **150000** Interval: **20000**

What You Have To Do

Assessment Objectives		
3c	6	Do **not** display a legend on this graph.
3e, 3f	7	Add a linear trendline to the graph. Display the trendline equation in the top left corner of the plot area, above the trendline.
3g	8	Insert a text box with the information below. Place it in the top right corner of the plot area.
		SOUTH – PERIOD TOTALS
4a, 4c, 4d, 4g, 4h	9	Apply the house style.
	10	Save the chart.
5a	11	Print your bar chart in **landscape** orientation.

TASK 4

Prepare a report comparing the period bookings in 2001 with period bookings in 2002.

What You Have To Do

Assessment Objectives		
1a	1	Open the file **ttlbooks**. Save it using your program's file type.
1e, 2d	2	Create a **line-column** graph showing the PERIOD TOTAL figures for 2001 and 2002. Use the line for the 2001 data series and columns for the 2002 data series.
3a	3	Use the title: **QUARTERLY BOOKINGS 2001–2002** Use the x axis title: **QUARTER** Use the y axis title: **INCOME (£)**
3d	4	Format the **y** axis as follows:
		Minimum value: **0** Maximum value: **200000** Interval: **50000**
3b	5	The x axis labels should be **QUARTER 1**, **QUARTER 2**, **QUARTER 3**, and **QUARTER 4**.
3c	6	Display a legend on this graph.
4a, 4c, 4d, 4f, 4g, 4h	7	Apply the house style.
	8	Save the chart.
5a	9	Print your chart in **landscape** orientation.